The Empty Nest Companion

...a little book of love and encouragement for when your child leaves the nest...

Briget Bishop,
Certified Professional Coach (CPC)

Susan Gross,
Certified Professional Coach (CPC)

Copyright © 2018
Briget R. Bishop, Susan M. Gross

This book is not intended as a substitute for the medical advice of physicians. The reader should regularly consult a physician in matters relating to his/her health and particularly with respect to any symptoms that may require diagnosis or medical attention.

ISBN-13: 978-1984001306
ISBN-10: 1984001302

Dedication

This Book is dedicated to all the moms and dads who raised a child to adulthood and gave them wings to fly!

Coach Briget: To God, who loves and strengthens me each and every day. To my daughters, Maureen and Tori. My greatest joy has been watching the two of you grow into powerful, loving, and compassionate women who are making a positive difference in this world. And to Lisa McGowan, my oldest and dearest friend: I dedicate this book to our incredible friendship and love over the years, and for your strong spirit, incredible support, and amazing capacity to love.

Coach Susan: I dedicate this book to the two greatest joys in my life—my sons, Jake and Zach, who continue to amaze and inspire me every day. I am so grateful for the wonderful relationship that we have and for the amazing young men that they have both become. Being a mom is, and always will be, the best part of my life. I also dedicate this book to all the moms and dads who have or will be navigating this phase of life, in hopes that they will find their way through this transition.

Foreword

Thank you, Susan and Briget, for selecting me to write the foreword for your book. I know it's going to help so many people! One of my main niches as a Coach is "Women who *finally* want to put themselves first." For many wives and mothers, they've been putting others first for so many years. It's an admirable way to live, but it can be draining and exhausting. I'm glad this book will inspire women of any age to live fully. As I like to say, having a self-wish is *not* selfish!

I love that the authors look at an Empty Nest with gratitude. It's something I know a thing or two about, and when we use it—in this situation or any other challenging scenario—we can see the positives and shift our energy. That's a great way to live.

Susan and Briget share wise insights in the book, and I highly encourage you to read it. Being present is important. We can't change the past, and worrying about the future is often not beneficial. I can't empathize with what it's like to be an Empty Nester mom, but I can say I'm all about hope and living in the present with gratitude. I love my adult relationship with my mother (Diane Terry), and I think she'd say the same. I'm optimistic/confident your kids have the same outlook!

Russ Terry

Author of:
My Gratitude Journal
Our Gratitude Mission
Our Gratitude Mission 2

Acknowledgements

We offer a heartfelt thank you to the moms who contributed their personal stories and journeys while going through the Empty Nest period. These women recognized the strength that came from within themselves and used it to navigate these unchartered waters. We hope you are as inspired and enlightened as we were by their stories.

There are only two lasting bequests we can hope to give our children.
One of these is roots, the other, wings.

~ Johann Wolfgang von Goethe

Table of Contents

We find delight in the beauty and happiness of children that makes the heart too big for the body.

~Ralph Waldo Emerson

Introduction

You have picked up this book, so chances are you are wondering what you can do with these unexplained feelings of loneliness and sadness since your children left the nest. We were in the exact same place. We understand. We have been there (and continue to be there), and want to help you on this journey.

We are both Certified Professional Life Coaches *and* Empty Nesters who initially started coaching each other through our Empty Nest emotions. This quickly morphed into a decision to write a book offering hope and inspiration to parents experiencing the stage of life when their children leave home. Aptly called "The Empty Nest," this season is indeed analogous to birds leaving the nest. It is a term that has been used widely to describe this phase of life for parents.

The intent of this book is not meant to replace counseling or professional help, but rather to provide some insight into the emotions, setbacks, and even triumphs a few of us have experienced while navigating the Empty Nest.

In the pages that follow, you will hear from other mothers whose sons or daughters left home. Through these stories—our own and those of six other women, you will learn that you are neither alone nor going crazy, and that life as you knew it has not ended, but is simply transforming. The stories are complemented by strategies and positive reflections to help you traverse this unknown territory. Know that there is hope and an amazing future during this season of your life!

So Many Feelings, So Much Change: How Do You Navigate It All?

An Empty Nest. What exactly is it, and how do you describe it to people who have not gone through it? For us, it was life altering. We realized that this journey we embarked upon within our families was multi-dimensional. It was hard to describe to those who hadn't experienced it. We went through the journey at different times in our lives and cannot say that one gender leaving the nest is easier than the other. Susan has two sons and Briget has two daughters, and we were impacted similarly, as well as differently. What we can say, however, is that it affected our lives in immeasurable ways.

No matter why your child is no longer part of your "nest" (i.e., graduated high school and moved out, left for college, graduated college and started a career, joined the military, etc.) the absence of him or her in your daily life is the same. For many of us, it just hurts. We miss them and the life we had when they were under our roof.

We've found that dealing with our emotions regarding the Empty Nest is a process, and although we each process differently, one common thread appears: we want our old lives back—to when our children lived with us and we dealt with the craziness of juggling life and its many commitments. Yet we need to reconcile that those days are in the past, and no matter how hard we wish for them to return, they won't.

It's a hard truth that we should face with strength, love, and gratitude to move forward to the next phase of our lives, which is enjoying and loving our children under new circumstances. Detaching from the past does not mean that we forget it; we simply make room for new memories and experiences, both for ourselves and our children.

Look Back but Move Forward
Our job as parents never ends, but it does shift based on our children's needs. Although we may long for the days when our children were

young and we were the center of their universe, let's remember that just because they are young adults doesn't mean that they don't need us. They do, but in a different way. We can still nurture them, but we have to learn how to nurture differently because they are going through a transition too!

Remember when your kids were little and you put them safely in their car seat? Yes, you were the parent/caretaker, always mindful of their safety and needs. Then some 16 years go by, and they are in the driver's seat alongside you, preparing for their driver's permit! And then in a blink of an eye, they have their driver's license and are now driving you around. This analogy is similar to that of the years preceding the Empty Nest; we are there, day in and day out in our kids' lives...helping, nurturing, navigating, and protecting. As time marches on, our involvement wanes as our kids gain their independence. We are glad of this independence. After all, isn't this the goal of parenting? But when this reality hits us— and it hits hard sometimes—we are left with great emptiness, which can include questions about our own self-worth. Since many of us define ourselves as being a mom/parent first and foremost, once our children don't need us, what are we to do with ourselves?

So with the car analogy, rather than being the 24/7 caregiver, protector, and nurturer to our children strapped safely in their car seats...we are now the passenger in *their* car...the passenger in *their* adult life. Hopefully as their passenger, you will still have many rides together, but it will be different, and that can be the hard part. This is because the shift is now their journey, and we need to be mindful that our preparations led them to this moment. So, rather than rejecting this new phase of life because it hurts, we need to understand it is OK to miss them and the old nest life while learning how to move forward and embrace this change.

Take Charge of Your Thoughts

During this navigation, you might encounter emotional lows filled with negativity, questioning whether you did enough as a parent and where you now fit into your child's life. Rather than dwell on the negative, try replacing these thoughts with gratitude. For example, if you find yourself miserable because the house is devoid of the daily chaos from when your child/children were there, take a breath and say, "I am so grateful for the opportunity to have raised an amazing son/daughter, and I am so proud of their achievements." Recognize the negative thought (and we know some of our minds can go into hyper-drive with a multitude of thoughts/ideas that drive us crazy), stop it in its tracks, and put a positive thought in its place.

Try to remember that everything begins with a thought. Really, just a thought. Here is an example: Years ago, Briget went to a nursing conference in Virginia. Before the main speaker came to deliver her presentation, a young man addressed the crowd. He walked out on stage with a blank canvas and three-color paints—black, white, and green. As he began his talk, he shared that he had two young sons, both under age 10. He spoke, then paused and painted on his canvas, then returned to talking to the audience. This went on for about 15 more minutes—he intermittently talked and painted. The audience sat in amazement, and yet no one could figure out the painting. The man then asked, "How many nurses in the room feel they are creative?" Fewer than a third of them raised their hands. "Hmm," he said, and then asked, "Do you know the difference between a creative person and one who is not creative?" His answer has stuck with Briget to this day. He said the difference is the creative person "thinks" he is creative. What? Let that sink in. The difference between a creative person and a non-creative person is the creative person just "thinks" he is creative.

The man continued to work on his painting, but the audience still did not know what it was. Then he did something dramatic—he rotated the painting 180°. Believe it or not, it was the Statue of Liberty. He had actually painted the entire thing upside down. Wow! Who would have ever thought of doing something that creative?

You must be wondering how this ties into the Empty Nest. Well, here it is. Your entire Empty Nest experience is how you choose to "think" about it. The difference will always come down to our thoughts. We can choose to think about scarcity or abundance. We can put our thoughts toward the fact that we will not have our children at home anymore nor be part of their day-to-day activities. We can also choose to think about how incredible it will be to create a brand-new future with them based on new experiences, new challenges, new joys, and a whole new paradigm in order to create a deeper and more engaging relationship with our children. The choice is completely ours. That is powerful, that is transformative, that is just plain cool. Think a little differently, and see what beautiful memories you can create with your children to enrich, embolden, and enliven your current relationship with them into something completely new and even more beautiful. It all starts with a positive thought!

Expect Less, Plan More

Those navigating an Empty Nest need to consider expectations, and how they can shape our experiences in this phase of life. Not all expectations are necessarily good or bad, but when we set expectations and life falls short of attaining them, we set ourselves up for frustration and disappointment. Setting realistic expectations in this new family dynamic is critical.

For example, expecting a spouse to fill the void puts all the heavy lifting on him or her, and when they fall short of meeting this expectation, resentment and disappointment quickly follow. Understanding your spouse, your relationship, and all their uniqueness helps to set attainable expectations. For example, your spouse may do a lot of business travel, and therefore is unable to be there for you at certain times when you need him/her the most. Rather than expecting your spouse to fill the void, create a "date night" for the two of you to enjoy once a week.

Similarly, staying in touch with your child who has left the nest is likely important, but expecting to talk to him or her on the phone every day is a lot to ask. Discussing the frequency of calls and visits with them ahead of time will help to alleviate feeling left out and alone. For example, instead of feeling dismissed when they choose not to pick up the phone, ask them to text you a smiley face emoji. This lets you know your child is OK and provides them with the space they might need. Although this is a different type of interaction than you originally hoped for, your expectation of hearing from your child is still met. Remember, their shift isn't necessarily "away from you", but rather "toward them" becoming more confident and independent. This is what you prepared them for, and it's a testament to the great job you did as a parent!

There might be days that your child relies heavily on you as they enter their independent adult phase; embrace these moments as small but wonderful signals that you are always needed in your child's life, just in a different way. Being nimble in this new relationship discovery process is essential, as there will be new external factors that can influence it, such as your child's new job/life responsibilities, or possibly a new love interest. You might need to revise communication with your adult child, whether it be how often to talk/text or how often to visit with them. By respecting their space while voicing what you need, you can hopefully reach a balance that works for everyone.

Please note, this expectation exercise is not about removing expectations, but rather being more realistic so as not to set yourself up for constant disappointment when they are not met. Being fluid with your expectations is important. Life changes constantly, and it's easier to go with the flow and alter your expectations accordingly, rather than expecting a certain event/behavior in order to be happy. You have the choice of defining and finding your happiness, and it should not be at the mercy of others not meeting unrealistic expectations.

Accept Your Feelings

Learning how to be nimble through change is important during this Empty Nest process, as it is also part of setting realistic expectations. We get it...the damned emptiness and quietness of the house just hurts sometimes! But beating ourselves up over it is not going to change the reality of our child moving on, and that's where being emotionally agile comes in. Accepting the changes and emotions that come with this transition helps with embracing the new reality—fighting it is draining. There will indeed be days when you feel great with the newfound freedom of not having to do five loads of laundry...and then there will be days that you'd give anything to do that extra load of laundry. There will be triggers that cause that roller coaster to make a million dips, like not being able to spend a birthday together because of the distance. But by being emotionally agile, one can learn new ways to manage the relationship based on this new reality. By acknowledging and accepting the Empty Nest, the parent-adult relationship presents wonderful opportunities to develop and grow.

From our perspective as coaches, we are here to validate your feelings. They are real, messy, and sometimes very raw. Learning to accept this new phase of life can be daunting and emotionally draining, but you are not alone, and no one is judging how long it takes you to maneuver through your emotions. Just like grief is a personal journey, so is this. In fact, the Empty Nest journey is akin to grieving. We grieve the loss of the life we loved when our kid(s) was/were under the same roof. It's important to give yourself the necessary time and space to understand your emotions. May you find comfort in knowing that many of the emotions, questions, and even doubts you are experiencing are shared by the women with whom we have spoken—those who have shared their stories here.

Where we love is home, home that our feet may leave, but not our hearts.

~Oliver Wendell Holmes

A Note About Our Story Contributors

When we sought story contributions, we ended up with 100% of the interest being from moms. Although we did not set out to include only women in our book, we found that they are the most vocal regarding their Empty Nest experiences. To guide them with their story contributions, we asked the women to answer the seven questions noted below. As coaches, we felt these questions helped to narrow down the multitude of feelings during this major transition, as well as provide some consistency in the information, allowing us to identify common threads, emotions, and themes being experienced.

The Empty Nest Questions:

1. Describe what it was like for you the first few days after your child moved out of the house? Please include their age at the time and why they moved

out (i.e.: college, joined the military, etc.)

2. What was the most difficult emotion/ experience for you when your child/ children moved out? What emotions did you experience that you did not anticipate?

3. If applicable, how did your significant other handle the Empty Nest change?

4. Did you feel supported by family and friends during this time? If so, who were you able to confide in and gain support from?

5. What did you do to get through your Empty Nest emotions? What are/were your coping skills?

6. If you are now adjusted to the Empty Nest life, please describe how you feel now, and what actions/activities you did to over-come your emotions (i.e.: new job; new hobbies; joined support groups)?

7. What would you tell your younger self had you known ahead of time how this would impact you in such a significant way? What would you have done differently?

Diane's Empty Nest
Welcome to the Old Soul Mother's Club
Diane (age 54), three children (ages 15, 17, 19)

Waking up that fateful morning, my feet did not want to touch the floor. Planting my feet firmly on the ground indicated that I was giving in to the moment that I had been so long avoiding. I felt unsteady, unsure of my footing. I had to think hard to move each muscle because they were fighting me. But moving at all showed that I was forwarding myself toward the events of the day that I had so long wished would not come. Not yet. It cannot be. How did time vanish so quickly? I sluggishly put one foot in front of the other and walked downstairs to prepare one more breakfast, something that I had done robotically for so long, going through the motions that had been ingrained in my mother role for 18 years. I walked into the kitchen and was greeted by my son, my first of three children. He sheepishly said, "Good Morning, Mom," as he has said countless times before. But that day, it was different. It was a "Good Morning, Mom" like no other, words loaded with heaviness, excitement, and anticipation of the new days to come. This was the day my son was going to college. Somehow I managed to muster a weak, "Good Morning, sweetie." I gave him a hug like no hug before, and the tears began, and they continued to flow on and off for several weeks as I moved through this new chapter of my life—my children leaving home, leaving me.

My son left our nest to embark on what millions of 18-year-olds do every year—their journey on to the next phase of their life. Except this moment was different from any other that the millions of mothers, fathers, and caregivers go through, given the same set of circumstances. For this was *my* child leaving. *My* boy separating from *me* and our unique connection that we had fostered over the last 18 years. As you are reading this, I am sure you feel empathy for my words, and it would certainly comfort me to know that you too are saying, "I understand what you are feeling. I have been through this." Or "I am about to experience this myself." Yes, this is true. But my child is my own unique experience, as your child is yours, and I felt so alone at that moment.

I was warned years ago from those mothers who trudged this path before me, those I ran into at the park as I strolled my beautiful baby around. Those old soul mothers, as I like to call them, who had that secret that only old soul mothers know to be true because they were here in my shoes when their children were little. At the moment of encountering these mothers, their own memories flooded back to them, remembering their days of being a new mom, and all the joys, amazing discoveries, and pure love of having this little being to nurture, these many moments that were only a blink of an eye ago. These old soul mothers reminisced in their minds about the treasured moments in their memory banks, kept quiet until they erupted to the surface in that old soul mother moment as she encountered my freshman new mother moment. We chattered away, our small mother talk. These old soul mothers always ended our conversation by saying, "Honey, enjoy these moments because it goes so fast." I chuckled at these statements, for I stood before them with my fruit juice and dried oatmeal-spotted shirt, my tired three-hours-of-sleep-a-night eyes, and I thought to myself, "Not fast enough!" But now, in the twilight hour before my first-born leaves me, a secret has been revealed. I am now an official old soul mother. I am part of that exclusive club. I have lived through these amazing light-speed years of watching my children grow and being part of their lives. Nothing prepares you for this moment of leaving the nest. Maybe I should have listened more intently to those words years ago: "Honey, enjoy these moments because it goes so fast." That was my warning bell, my preparatory red flag that they waved before my eyes. These were the pearls of wisdom to which maybe I should have been more attuned. These mothers whom I met on those random encounters were trying to tell me to really, really enjoy every last second of time with my children. These women who walked before me were my beacons of light, but I was too caught up in my fresh new-mother moments to understand what they were trying to tell me.

My three amazing children have been the

greatest gift in my life, and I have had the privilege of staying home with them these past 18 years. I never thought that I would be a stay-at-home mother. I wanted it all, a career and motherhood. But when I held my first-born for the first time, everything changed. I felt whole. With each additional child, my being was more complete. I call my children my greatest gift because I unfortunately had my own gift of a mother taken away way too soon. My mother died when I was 10 years old, and a brother followed in death when I was 22. Abandonment was something that I knew too well. People leave you—it's a hard fact of life that I experienced way too early, and it left me with a fear that has been over-whelming at times in my life.

My mantra became "I better depend on my-self, for you never know if you can depend on that person in your life to be there for you." There had always been a void in me. It was an emptiness that I never could quite fill, even with a wonderful marriage, family, friends, and other life joys that surround me. You fill that void some, but never completely. But then, my children came, three beautiful beings that filled this void that had been unfillable for so many years.

I am experiencing loss again. Thankfully, this is not the type of trauma that I encountered in my past, but it is a loss. I know how to do this. I must mourn this. I must go through these stages, feel the pain and sadness in order to come out stronger. I call on my core, my own essence, that compass that somehow guided me through all those other difficult moments in my life. I was able to move through those moments of loss in my past, and I know that I will get through this moment too. I have to feel this sadness now in order get to my final destination of happiness and contentment again. I say to myself, "I am resilient. I will not break. I will move through this transition with grace and the anticipation of waiting to see how my children further develop." How do I do this? How do I not break? How can I see all the wonderful anticipatory moments of what is to come as my children grow, instead of focusing on all that is gone?

Those first several weeks were hard. I walked past his room and just stared in, imagining him sitting at his desk. I sat on his bed and quietly took in the space that he once occupied. I allowed myself to feel this sadness for a few days. But then I knew that I had to get moving again. I could not stay in this state for long because it would take over my being, and I was not going to let it do that. I made plans with fellow mom friends, and we talked about our feelings and supported one another. I threw myself into my favorite pastimes of gardening and art. My husband and I planned weekend outings now that we had free time. I had more time to spend with my other children for fun activities. We kept a weekly Skype call with my son on the same day at the same time, and texting him has become my new best friend.

Life took on a new rhythm, and I found myself enjoying my new free chunk of time. I have two more children who will be leaving in the next three years, and I still have to focus on them. I realize that I need to pre-plan better for this, especially when my last child leaves. Some of my own pearls of wisdom that I am working to incorporate into my life can be yours too, such as:

Find what you loved about raising your children. Really figure out which aspects gave you joy, enrichment, and energy, whether it was just being around them, helping out with all those art projects, coaching their sports team, or volunteering in some other area. Then find that particular activity and add it to your life. Become a volunteer with kids, begin that art class that you have been putting off, coach other children. Whatever it is, get it into your life before your child leaves because that will help to fill the void and better manage the transition.

Allow all the feelings that go along with this moment of your child leaving. You are mourning. It is a loss. Examine your feelings without fear. Feel the sadness, let the tears flow. You need to experience all feelings to come out stronger and find your new direction on the other side. Reach out to your fellow mom friends and support each other.

Rekindle your couplehood with your spouse or partner. This should be going on throughout your marriage, but as we all know, children become a priority and we might neglect this. Begin date nights again. Do not start this a few weeks before your child is leaving, but at least a couple years in advance, especially if your couplehood has been taken over by all the kids' activities.

Dream. Dream big. Dream little. Dream realistically, but dream of your future and what you want for it. If you would love to have that house at the beach, dream it. If you want that fancy car, dream it. Want to retire early? Dream it. Figure out what may be realistic for you and your partner, and make plans on how to achieve it. We all have to keep moving toward something that we hope for ourselves.

Looking back with wisdom is one of life's intentions. One may reflect on this when we are beyond that certain time that was momentous for whatever reason, and we find ourselves revisiting and looking at these memories with a fresh set of eyes. We are made aware of this when we embark on another meaningful moment in our lives, requiring self-reflection on past behaviors, feelings, and thoughts as to how to handle it differently. I look back on my journey as a mother, and I hold that old soul mother's secret. This is what I would do better: I would enjoy those precious moments, putting aside my own frustrations with my own lack of personal time when I was engaged for the umpteenth time with another game of Chutes and Ladders; playing with American Girl dolls; building Legos; making 20 million snacks a day (at least it felt like that!); soothing a crying baby; the chaotic birthday parties; soiled pants and endless breast feeding; all those sporting events; the crazy juggling of activities shoved into a four-hour span; the drama of adolescence; and the push and pull of independence that we go through with our children as they grow.

I look back on my journey as a mother, and I can say with heartfelt confidence that I am a proud member of the Old Soul Mother's Club. The only club requirement is journeying through motherhood. I only became a member after experiencing many years of walking in the same shoes of my fellow club members. Our shoes are scuffed and full of holes, but they still carry us with our joys, heartaches, and unbounded love for our children. Now, when I pass a mother with young children, I have earned the privilege of sharing the secret that she will take on her own journey through motherhood. She will pass this little secret along to others when she becomes a true member of the Old Soul Mother's Club, and she will share these words with unflinching conviction to that new mom: "Honey, enjoy every moment because it goes so fast."

The Coaches' Insight: A key takeaway from Diane's story is learning to acknowledge and accept your emotions. They are real, they are yours, and they need to be honored as well as embraced. Diane was able to acknowledge her emotions without judgment and accept them; she even embraced the "Old Soul Mother's Club" notion in order to accept this new phase of life. It is possible to truly work through your emotions if you learn to accept them, however difficult they are.

Patrice's Empty Nest
What Now?! It's About Finding Yourself...
Patrice (age 51), two children (ages 24, 26)

My name is Patrice and I'm an empty nester! I don't believe there is a 12-step program for this, nor anything to prepare you for the shock. It's a shock that hits twice as hard if you are a single parent, and for me, it came earlier than most.

I always treasured and agreed with Khalil Gibran's philosophy on children: "Your children are not your children. They are the sons and daughters of Life's longing for itself. They come through you but not from you, and though they are with you yet they belong not to you."

That is just a portion of his poem, but one I have always strived to remember and live by.

I have two daughters, Erica and Carly, and they were born in that order about 17 months apart. They didn't have a traditional childhood by any means. I divorced their father while still pregnant with Carly and was a single mother until they were about 3 and 5, when I remarried.

After leaving my second husband of almost 10 years, I found the perfect house and was so excited to have this time just with my girls. We had countless sleepovers, went to concerts, visited NYC at least once a month to see a Broadway play, and went on many spontaneous road trips to various destinations—even some with no destination. They were truly the best years of my life. How was I to know how fast they would go?

When they were in middle school, I became disillusioned with the public school system, and moved them to a Sudbury Valley model school, which followed the philosophy that children naturally want to learn and will gravitate toward the interests best suited for them. I had not even thought about either of them graduating early, which they both did—at the ripe age of 16.

Erica was accepted at an out-of-state college

in Savannah, Georgia, where she was the youngest in her dorm. She did very well, but by the end of the year she decided that college was too expensive. At 17, she joined the Army to work on Black Hawks. By the time basic training and AIT were over, my 18-year-old baby was deployed to spend five years serving in the 82nd Airborne in Germany and Afghanistan.

My youngest graduated at the age of 16 as well. She worked at our local firehouse and had a day job, so she was gone the majority of the time. She started dating a longtime friend who was also firefighter, and at the ages of 17 and at 18, they were married. He had joined the Air Force in the interim, and they were whisked away to Fort Campbell, Kentucky. She completed nursing school there, and they now live in Washington State, where she is an emergency room nurse.

So within the span of two years, both of my girls were gone. And not just up the street gone, but out-of-the-state and out-of-the-country gone! I could neither see nor call them every day because they had extremely busy lives. While I was very proud of them in every way and happy for the amazing journeys upon which they each fearlessly embarked, I was definitely left empty.

Not an empty nest, because they both left a ton of crap at my house, but an empty heart and life. Not in a dramatic sense, but in the sense that my entire life revolved around getting them to and from school, making breakfast, lunch, and dinner, getting them to and from doctors and dentists, and every day of my life was spent either doing or planning to do something for one or both of them.

I was left with my head spinning and asking myself, "What now?" I realized that even though I knew this day would come eventually, I never had a plan for me, for what I wanted to do and be when they finally ventured off to their own lives.

That was my biggest mistake, not planning for the future me. The most important thing I'd tell my younger self is to have a plan for my life once my kids got on with living theirs. They were super busy, and I didn't want to invade their lives; I wanted them to be the amazing, self-sufficient adults I raised them to be, and they could not be that if I was constantly bothering them.

After my girls left, I dated a man with two daughters for five years. They stayed with us every other weekend, so that filled in some time, but again, I even let that take away from figuring out who and what I wanted to be now that I was free.

Here I am almost 10 years later, and I have a grandson. Erica and her husband live back in our home state and attend college on the GI bill. I am the primary caregiver for my grandson, Nik, and I finally know what I want to do with my life. I want to write children's books, and Nik has inspired me to do just that. Maybe sometimes what we are meant to do finds us because we never found it!

Bottom line: realize that one day you will look around and find all of your children gone. Start thinking now about how you want to spend that time. What things bring you joy, a sense of purpose, meaning to your life? Find those things and do them. You will be happier, and so will your children.

The Coaches' Insight: A key takeaway from Patrice's story is listening; and in this situation it is learning to "be still" and listen to your inner voice, as that is usually where the answer is...within you! For Patrice, it was knowing that something needed to fill the void left by the empty nest, yet she couldn't figure out what that was or looked like. By simply observing and feeling what "felt right," the answer came to her—embark on writing children's books. We all need a purpose, and this goal turned out to be not just a purpose but a passion!

Pam's Empty Nest
SAHM (Stay-At-Home Mom) to Empty Nest
Pam (age 59), 4 children (ages 26, 28, 30, 32)

Facing our empty nest was not as easy as people told me it would be. "Oh, don't worry," they promised. "It gets easier with each child. By the time the youngest is ready, you will hardly be able to contain yourself!" Ha! Those were bold-faced lies! It actually got harder with each daughter—did I mention I have four? What happens is with each child's departure, one becomes very aware of what this truly means—your baby is not only gone, she is not coming back and an entire era has ended. Don't get me wrong. I am very proud of my daughters, and I tried very hard to raise them to be independent. But it really smacks you in the face when you have been successful!

By the time the youngest was ready to go off to college, I was an emotional wreck. I had spent the last 25 years raising daughters. My husband and I decided upon the birth of our first child that it would be best for one of us to stay home and raise our children even though it would mean doing without certain things such as a big house, a new car, and clothing from stores other than Walmart and Kmart, etc. So for 23 years, I stayed home and raised the kids. Actually, staying home is something one rarely does while raising children. I spent a quarter of a century volunteering, chauffeuring, managing, doctoring, nurturing, encouraging, making priceless memories, laughing until it hurt, praying, and creating family traditions—a good deal of which took place outside the home—at school, gymnastics, piano and cello lessons, soccer games/practices, band, dance team, competition dance, chorus, softball, and so on.

I gave my best effort at preparing myself for the fact that the nest would be empty at some point in time. I talked about it, joked about it, and tried to envision what my life would be like when the last of our precious ones left the nest. I had nothing on which to base my theories other than a desperate attempt to prepare for and come to terms with the reality that would be mine. I entertained thoughts of going to the movies alone without taking out a second mortgage when taking the entire family. I envisioned long walks on the beach without having sand thrown on me or keeping a watchful eye on children in the water. I considered a bit of traveling without having to entertain the girls, break up fights, or answer the age old question, "Are we there yet?"— *five hundred thousand times!* I anticipated quiet and calm days and nights without interruption from a frightened, sad, or energetic child. I dreamed of room renovations and a house that, once it was cleaned up, stayed that way for longer than a second. I talked about having my own agenda again instead of having every minute dictated by my daughters' schedules. Yes, I considered, thought, shared, discussed, and I thought, prepared myself nicely. Even so, when the reality of an empty nest hit, it hit hard. *Everything* stopped. *Everything*. And I realized that what an empty nest left me was ample time.

I would not change a single minute of those 23 years other than two things: find a way to make money while staying at home raising the kids, and discovering a secret way to prolong the inevitable empty nest. At first, I felt as though I had been laid off from a job I loved. I went from being busy every second of the day to having nothing to do, cold turkey. During that first year of an empty nest, I set out to fill the empty hours.

When I thought about it, there were plenty of chores I could finally get around to starting, but I decided the first thing I needed to do was get a puppy. I was right. He's certainly the love of my life, and we do just about everything together. It's not that I thought he would be a good replacement for the kiddos, but I knew he would keep me occupied, and that's exactly what I needed. The first year of my empty nest was spent filling my time with yard work, which I had neglected the entire time raising the kids. I tried organic gardening, where I discovered I had nothing even remotely resembling a green thumb. I then tried organizing the gazillion pictures I had taken over the years as well as scrapbooking, which took three months but served as productive therapy. Getting in shape happened and "unhappened" about five times in the first three years of the nest emptying out, and it's still an ongoing success/fail story. Next, I started a blog, which was frightening but one of the best things I've ever done (right up there with getting the dog). I took up hobbies—specifically, bird watching and photography—which I still enjoy, and knitting, which was fun but wore itself out after a year. I purged the house of all the junk and I discovered it's endless. I reconnected with old friends and sought advice from present friends. I enlightened myself spiritually. I even redecorated rooms.

A word of warning on the last one: once you redecorate and get organized, one or more of your precious now adult kids is going to move back into your house. And it's not necessarily going to be pretty. As a matter of fact, it may make you wonder why you missed them in the first place.

The level of busy in the first year was so intense it left me exhausted. The drive died down. I had thrown myself into it full force and ran out of juice. The good news is that the business of finding ways to fill the hours kept me from sitting around lamenting about the nest being empty. I never felt like the situation was hopeless or that I would not adjust. Nevertheless, when the first year ended, I needed something else. My friends had jobs to keep them busy, so I decided it would be a good idea to go to the elementary school that my daughters attended and volunteer once again. Eventually, this led to a tutoring job, and then a teaching position, which kept many hours filled. As a stay-at-home mom, there was really no time to sit still. Even at night my "mommy brain" had a section that stayed alert for even the slightest out-of-place sound. While the girls were at school, time did not slow down, and I didn't either. I was up at their school volunteering in the office and classrooms. During the summer, we hit the beach or a park every day. Even through high school, the busyness continued. There is a different sort of busy when the nest empties out—the kind that you can complete in a few hours, and then you find yourself left with *time*. Alone time. Solitary confinement. And it doesn't help if you realize the man you are left with is not someone with whom you still want to spend time.

I know I am not alone in this boat, and I'm sure the reasons for these feelings are many. In my case, it was a long time coming. It's easy to overlook certain undesirable behaviors, even the toxic ones, when your time is filled with all things kid-related. Once the last one leaves the nest, however, you are left with not only empty hours to fill, but also some stark realizations that were left on the back burner for a couple decades. My situation includes emotional abuse and neglect with a little alcoholism thrown in for good measure. These things were not difficult to deal with when the girls were little. I was focused on raising them and didn't really concern myself with much else except the drinking. Luckily, most of that took place with his sister or friends, and not in the house. Once the girls got older, he started backing off from the obvious drinking and actually stopped for a long time. However, so much damage was done over the years that I simply had no interest reviving the relationship once everyone was out of the nest.

Looking back, I wish I would have taken on a job in which I could stay home and work. I didn't consider that I would want out after the nest emptied, so at this point, I am stuck financially. I think these young moms who have online shops and/or blogs that make money are so smart. If they're lucky in love, they'll have travel money or fix-up-the-house money when their kids move on, and if they aren't, they'll have "moving-on" money. I did take a teaching job, but I also decided to quit that after seven years to stay home with my granddaughter, which was agreeable to everyone. Once I was home with her, I opened my own online shop and am working to get myself into a good financial position.

There are people who assume certain things are true of empty nesters, like they are able to handle having an empty nest because they are financially sound or have amazing loving relationships with their spouses. Yet, I've seen those very people have a worse time than I had as the nest emptied. Some folks believe women in an abusive relationship do harm to their kids. But life is not black and white. Abuse of any form knows no boundaries. It's never as simple as just removing yourself from the situation. I am educated. I have undergraduate degrees in sociology and psychology and an MS in Early Childhood Development. I am not lazy. I worked through college and grad school, and I worked until my first daughter was born. I have counseled women in an unofficial manner about dealing with and getting out of abusive relationships. I knew better, but I did not do better. I was more concerned with raising my girls than worrying about my relationship with my spouse. I am also dealing with severe anxiety and depression, both of which developed over the course of the marriage. Neither are an excuse, but simply facts that make life decisions more difficult than not.

Instead of having a pity party, I tried seeking advice from friends whom I discovered were in the same boat as I was with their spouses. They have been successful in adjusting to their relationships with their spouses, not being intimate in any way and living together as roommates. They attend family functions together, and some are grandparents and enjoy their grandkids together. It can be done if that is all you want from a spousal relationship. One thing that came out of these discussions was starting the online shop, and I have distanced myself from my husband as much as possible. Sorting out an unhealthy spousal relationship is much more difficult than facing the kids growing up and moving out.

Except maybe for one thing: boomerang kids. I've had two. That phase left me with a true appreciation and longing for an empty nest. When adult children move back in, they bring their new annoying habits with them, coupled with the behaviors of which you were not fond when they lived with you the first time around. The first one moved back after graduating college just until she found a job, which took two years. During the second year, her oldest sister moved back. That took three years. I was a nervous wreck. The rooms I redecorated and set up as a guest room and study were taken over in the blink of an eye. Our family is split, with three of them being the messiest people on the face of the earth and three of us being almost OCD about being neat and tidy. Guess who moved back in with me? Yep. The two who are messy like their dad. They also came back expecting me to be the chief cook and bottle washer, but at least they did their own laundry.

My life's roller coaster has it all. The steep climbs up followed by the straight drops down, the loops, the turns, the tunnels...but my favorite parts are few and far between— the lulls. Those uneventful times when everything goes smoothly. When the people around you and even the world outside stop causing a ruckus, and you can just relax enough to enjoy and appreciate life. When your personal space is respected and things are quiet, calm, peaceful. When adult kids move back home, the lull is disturbed.

When you spend 20+ years raising four daughters, you not only want some down-time, you deserve it. You should be able to enjoy being still and quiet. You should be able to enjoy a clean and tidy house. You should no longer have interruptions at every turn. You should be able to buy groceries and not have them disappear in just a couple of days. You should be able to put things in their place and find them right where you left them, when you need them. You should be able to have your drawers and closets left alone. You've spent decades having messes, noise, destruction, intrusions...not that they were bad things, but when you don't have it anymore, you realize you're exhausted. It takes time to relax from all that.

Most of us empty nesters get that time, until the kids move back in and stay for *years*. And the roller coaster's loops and steep climbs up and straight drops down are back. You realize you had less than a second on the lull that led you right into a fast, sharp turn followed by a steep up-ward climb. And then you spent the next years going round and round and up and down so fast that you cannot remember why in the world you liked the roller coaster of life when you were raising kids. Except that they were little then. Now that they're all grown up, whether you want to admit it or not, you have the expectation that they will be out on their own, or if they have moved back home, they will respect your ways. That does not happen. They move right back in, bringing their ways with them and expect you to adjust to them. Roller. Coaster. Loop.

Having adult kids move back in makes the straight, slow lulls a waiting game. Waiting for them to move back out and experience life as it should be experienced—by making your own way. Moving back in for a short period of time is one thing, but once a couple of years have passed, it becomes more of a burden, especially if you do not see anyone heading in the direction of getting up and moving on. Couple all of that with no partner in whom you can confide, and life gets really interesting really fast.

The hardest part of the empty nest for me was discovering how to fill the empty hours and learning how to deal with a spousal relationship I no longer wanted. I did not have a difficult time letting the girls go out on their own because that's what parenting is about. We are given these wonderful gifts for only a short time, and we raise them to be the best adults they can be. I did that and I loved every minute of it. However, once the nest emptied and I had adjusted, I came to cherish the quiet, calm, peace, and cleanliness.

If I were to advise my younger self, I would mention just a few things. First, if you stay home and raise the kids, find a way to also make your own money to benefit you, wheth-

A gift for you

Loren and Mike, Congratulations on seeing Anna off to Indonesia. We wish her the best time and we wish you a peaceful transition! From Coddington Design

er or not you want to stay with your spouse. Second, if you find yourself going through extreme withdrawals from the kids moving out, seek professional help. I've seen too many women not recovering from something to which they should have been able to adjust. Third, take care of yourself. Take a minute here and there to enjoy friends and do something healthy. Fourth, you are allowed to be happy, and if you aren't, find the path and follow it. Finally, raise the kids not only to go out in the world, but to stay out there!

Our empty nests are inevitable. I find it best to view it as an adjustment period, which helps us realize the light is at the end of the tunnel. An empty nest is not the first adjustment period we've had in our lives, and it won't be the last. There is life in an empty nest, even if your partner isn't there for you. Find your center, focus, get help if you need it. Change your perspective from doom and gloom to a new and exciting phase. Everyone deserves happiness but it comes from within, and it's just sitting there waiting for you to notice it.

The Coaches' Insight: Although Pam initially struggled with the vast emptiness of the kids leaving, she refocused her energies on herself, which is amazing! By learning how to look forward (refocus), rather than just look backwards, she was able to find ways to bring happiness to herself. Through "peeling back the onion" without self-judgment, Pam was able to gain great insight into the decisions/choices she's made in life, especially how they impacted her future decisions.

Angela's Empty Nest
Empty Nest...Who Am I Now?
Angela (age 54),
four children (ages 23, 30, 32, 34)

Every mother's story is unique. I have a "yours, mine, and ours" family—children from my current husband's first marriage and my first and current marriages. Each child that left my nest embodied a different set of emotions. The feelings of losing my identity escalated with each child's exit.

Our oldest, my stepson Michael who is now 34 years old, lived with us from the age of 10. At the age of 14, he started to pull away from our family, spending alternating weeks with his mother. By the time he left the nest permanently, he already had his flight plan laid out, and we had adjusted to him not being around. I was not his biological mother, and I still had my hands full with three others at home—two daughters from my first marriage of 10 years, and one from my current marriage. It was actually a nice transition. I was firmly wrapped up in my career as a secretary and registrar at a middle school and running my household. Michael did not move out of state, so we could see him whenever we wanted. A few years later he married and acquired a three-year-old stepdaughter, and soon I had beautiful new grandchildren to cuddle!

Cassie, my oldest child, is two years younger than Michael. My independent, free-spirited, and slightly rebellious-from-birth child, now at age 32, she has multiple tattoos and cotton candy-colored hair. She is also a yogi and owns her own successful jewelry business. Although I knew she would push her way through life with gusto, it was still difficult for me to drive home after leaving her at the college dorm, only an hour away. I remember making it to the halfway point on our drive home, and I cried the rest of the way. What upset me was not so much my role changing, but more that I would miss her lively spirit in our home. I missed her, but I was busy at home with two more children. She still needed me periodically. Money was always tight. It was always a war for her dad and her stepdad to cough up spending money for her. I spent so much time as the middleman, in the tangle of finances and hurt feelings, that time flew by. She spent little time at home during her college years, working a lot because of the money situation. Cassie finished college, taught art for a couple of years, and then married a wonderful man and moved to Arizona. It was difficult, but we all eventually adjusted. We all sucked in our emotions and moved forward.

My daughter Chelsea was two years behind Cassie. She is my social butterfly and also my love bug—always a snuggly one. Chelsea had a large core group of friends who were together since their middle school years. Many of them played basketball together for years. Now age 30, all of the members of this core group are still together. Chelsea roomed in college with her friends and stayed in apartment complexes after college with them too. Many of them have returned to their hometown to raise their families and live in the same neighborhood. Though she assured me verbally that she always needed me, I knew better. She would be fine. She relied more on her friends than anyone else. She was the easiest to let fly; she had been flying since her freshman year of high school. I missed her. I missed going to her basketball games, and I missed her sweet hugs and cuddles. Chelsea graduated, has a great job, and will soon be married to a great guy. She also stayed in the state. This was getting more difficult, but I still had one at home.

Allyson, age 23, is seven years behind the rest and the "ours" portion of the "yours, mine, and ours" scenario, the child I had with my husband, Jack. This is where it started to get ugly! There had always been a buffer each time a child took flight, but there will be no buffer when Allyson leaves. She has always been my homebody. Through her college years, she called, texted, and Snapchatted multiple times a day. She came home every weekend from college to spend time with us and spent her summer and spring breaks with us. Her sisters reprimanded her for coming home so much. They told her, "It will make it harder for Mom and your dad to adjust after you leave!" They are correct, but who does not want to come home to Friday movie night and Dad's Sunday morning waffles and bacon? Allyson tried to stay away but was unsuccessful. I like to think it is because she needs me, but unfortunately, it is partially because she knows that I am walking a tightrope—and she holds one end of the rope. She has seen firsthand my breakdowns, when I "lose it" over ridiculous things. I hope and pray that she sees that I am becoming stronger every day.

The years that Allyson spent in college were a true test to my emotional stability. Cassie and Chelsea's grandmother on their dad's side died of cancer, and a month later their father died of a heart attack! The process of picking up the pieces of shrapnel was at times unbearable. No one wants to see a child go through something like that. In a darkened corner of my soul, that I have only spoken to my dear husband about, I secretly hoped that this event would work to my advantage and bring my girls closer to me. They even told me during the days of the viewing/funeral, "Mom, you are *it* now!" Woohoo! No one to compete with! I had them to myself! They are going to need me more now! In hindsight, I am appalled that I was that pathetic and selfish. I wanted so desperately to fix the grief for them. That is what a mother does! Children fall down, and you kiss the hurt and console them until the pain is gone, or until it is at least forgotten. Not only did I want to fix this, I wanted *them* to want me to fix it for them. I wanted them to call me and to want me to fill the void. If anything, I heard from them less in those horrible months after the funerals because they were so busy trying to pick up their own shrapnel. It was so pathetic that I expected my children to pick up *my* shrapnel as well their own. Cassie sought solace in grief counseling, her sister, and her husband. Chelsea leaned on Cassie and her boyfriend. Cassie and I urged her to go to grief counseling, but she did not feel the need or didn't want to take the time. I hugged them when I saw them, talked with Cassie on the phone, and even made a surprise visit across the country when I heard she was feeling extra down. I think there was only so much consoling I could do. I beat myself up to this day about things I said and didn't say during that time period. In hindsight, I look back on that year and realize that I really did raise strong girls. They both leaned on each other and still do to this day. Last year, on the anniversary of their dad's passing, they went on a sister trip to Hawaii together, one of their dad's favorite vacation spots. Did I want to be part of that? Yes, I wanted to be there with them! But I have learned that I don't share in that part of their life. How could I belong there? I could not fully understand their pain—both my parents are still living. During this dark time for everyone, I learned so much about myself, about grief, and how to let go of pieces of my grown children.

The years between Chelsea leaving home and the present was and is a black hole of emotions. It truly can only be compared to a roller coaster. There were periods that I felt emotionally strong and times that I bottomed out. The underlying current was the same: I was losing my title of "mom" as I have always known it, and why don't my children need me anymore? Allyson definitely needs me, which is wonderful, but only compounds the fact that the others obviously do not. What a mess. Allyson and my husband are having to take the brunt of my emotions and that makes me feel worse. I find myself telling the kids, "You don't really need me anymore!" I got all kinds of attention for that statement, but of course I felt extremely guilty afterward for stooping to that level. These years were and still are so sloppy and self-loathing. I feel like I am not in control of my emotions. I work in a middle school, and I equate these years of my life to the emotional disposition of a tween girl—having so many emotions and not knowing how to handle them, so you blurt out inappropriate things and cry about everything. I realized that it was a good time to seek some professional counseling. I didn't want to be that crazy mom who cannot keep herself together.

For me, counseling was helpful. My counselor was going through the same situation as I was, so we commiserated and came up with a plan. We agreed that more friends were needed. I needed to be more honest about my feelings with my daughters (without vomiting my emotions over them). I have put "Family Day" in place once a month. Everyone comes over one Sunday a month to hang out, eat, and play games. Every other week I have a set day that I get together with Chelsea. It is our special time together, and I cherish it. I needed to fill my time with things other than thinking about the old version of the definition of "mom" and begin reconstructing what it meant to be a mom to my grown children.

As I write this, I am sitting next to Allyson as she plans her wedding, after which she will be living in another state. I have worked diligently to put things in place to make the transition easier. I have developed many friendships over the last couple of years as preparation to fulfill my need to do things with other women. I feel sometimes that I am making replacements for my children, but in reality, they could never be replaced. Some of these girlfriends are empty nesters too. I have enjoyed making plans with my husband for his fast-approaching retirement. I have built in special times to get together on a regular basis with Chelsea, Michael, and their families who remain in the state of Indiana. I work on my physical health and try and keep my creative juices flowing through different crafts and music. My faith in God plays a constant underlying role in my life, so more involvement in my church is a given.

I know that this next year will be difficult no matter what prep work I have laid out. My last child will leave home in 37 days, 7 hours, and 33 minutes (but who's counting). I have made a solemn promise to try to hold my tongue when feeling emotional. Jack has been a stabilizing force thus far. He seems to understand now more than ever what I have been going through because his little girl is about to leave us. We will hold on tight to each other (literally and figuratively) over the final curves, hills, and valleys that the Lord has planned for our lives together. Grandchildren have already entered the picture, so hopefully many of those "hills" are more babies to love and spoil. We will travel, find new hobbies, and relax. We will watch our grown children maneuver through some of the same challenges that we did and, Lord willing, we will be around for them to come to us for advice. I will savor my friendships and find times to laugh and drink a little wine with them. I also look forward to retirement one day, and maybe I will have time to do some volunteer work. All in all, I cannot complain.

I consider that I am still going through this

transition in my life. I cannot say what it is like to be on the other side of this journey, though I can see the light at the end of the tunnel. In hindsight, I can see that the process is very slow and bumpy. At times I thought to myself, "I got this!" Next thing I knew, Jack and/or Allyson were helping me pick up the wreckage of another meltdown, which are usually spurred by an event—weddings, graduations, Christmas with an absent child, or something said or not said. I look back and can clearly see that I am doing better. I don't melt down over the little things as much. I pick and choose my battles. I know that I am needed in other ways. My grown daughters look forward to having babies and bringing them over for Grandma to spoil, and spoil them I will! They know that I will be there as support when babies are born and stay with them as long as they need their mom there.

So the dust is beginning to settle, and my children are all doing great. They are all college-educated, married (or soon to be), and are most importantly, kind. Isn't this what I strove for?

__The Coaches' Insight:__ Angela came to the realization that she was now needed as a mother in many different ways than what she had previously experienced. Recognizing that her journey had taken on a new direction was at first terrifying, but as Angela learned, it did not stop her. With time and lots of self-love, her role as once actively parenting her children took on a new meaning and trajectory—she was launched into a new and exciting untapped future with her grown children. By changing her perception, she was able to learn to adapt to the Empty Nest.

Michelle's Empty Nest
Life is Challenging, but There is Hope!
Michelle (age 47), two children (ages 21, 28)

I never thought being an empty nester would affect me as much as it has. I do not think that my story is unique or my kids being away from me makes my story special. But talking and writing about it makes me feel so much better.

I became a mother at a young age—I was only 19 when Allysa was born. Young and single parenting was not the way I envisioned my adult years to begin, but I made the choice, and I do not regret it at all.

It was just Allysa and me for a few years. At the age of three, she was diagnosed with epilepsy. She outgrew her seizures at the age of seven, but because her medication contained steroids, she gained a lot of weight. So we faced the weight-loss battle. I kept Allysa active as much as possible. She did tap and ballet and played soccer, and then she found her real passion—softball, which she played from age 7 to 15.

I was a busy mom. I worked full time, so Allysa was in afterschool care. I took her to softball practices and her games on Saturdays. Of course, I was team mom. She was also in Girl Scouts. On Sundays, we were active in our local Catholic church, where she went to Sunday School. Hard to believe that at the age of 26, I decided to do the whole single parent thing *again*…yes, I was pregnant. I made the choice to be a mom again, and of course I do not regret it.

This time, I gave birth to Christopher, who is seven years younger than Allysa. Boy, did I have my hands full. Allysa was not always the good big sister; she often resented Christopher and felt so many things were unfair. For instance, why did she have to empty the trash? Why didn't Christopher (who was a toddler) have the same chores? All Christopher wanted to do was follow Allysa around. He loved his sister.

Now with the two of them, I had to find an

activity for Christopher. Because Allysa was active in softball, I couldn't put Christopher in baseball. It was impossible. So, I had to toggle the sports. Christopher did fall soccer and Allysa spring softball. I was team mom for him as well, and he was a Cub Scout.

See? It's the typical busy mom story. I completely revolved my life around my kids and their activities. Every weekend had to do with their activities.

Things drastically changed when Allysa hit the age of 14; her seizures came back and they were different. She suffered from two different types of seizures, and it was so hard for her. The seizures affected her short-term memory and she struggled in school, going from being a straight-A student, to barely graduating high school. I devoted a lot of my time to her medical needs, and Christopher had to be the supportive brother. But he built up a lot of anger and resentment because of all the attention Allysa required, and how everything we did revolved around her needs.

As Allysa hit adulthood, her seizures worsened, and it became evident that I was clearly enabling her situation. She required brain surgery and depression set in. I was faced with the most difficult decision in my life—finding other living arrangements for her. Alyssa was very good at manipulating and guilting me into things, which led to a lot of fighting among Christopher, my new fiancé, and me. She knew how to push the right buttons, so that I allowed her to stay locked in her room or just lie around all day. So the hunt started to find her a group home or assisted living facility.

I was fortunate to find three great programs. One allowed Allysa to qualify for social security so she could have some income, and they provided free disabled services transportation. Another allowed her to volunteer and help other individuals with disabilities. The last program allowed her to live with a family who had rooms available for people who were "independent" but still required assistance in cooking and doctor's appointments. We interviewed several families before settling on that one. Allysa had a chance to be independent from me and learn how to cope with living without me doing everything for her.

I helped Allysa pack her belongings and made the drive (one mile away from me) to her new home. She didn't say a word. She was upset that this was happening. After she was settled, she went to her new room, closed the door behind her, and didn't say goodbye to me. I drove away, crying all the way home. I felt empty, like a failure.

As a mother, wasn't it my responsibility to take care of my children forever? With Allysa's epilepsy, couldn't I have done more to "fix" her (yes, I know...there is no cure). This is how I felt. I was unable to fix my baby girl, and now I was going to let another family take care of her. How could I? I couldn't dwell on my feelings. I had to focus my attention on my son, Christopher.

During all the time focusing on Allysa, my son struggled having me as a mother. He was so awful during his teen years, and I swore he hated me or at least I felt that way. Christopher had so much anger that was pent up from the years when Allysa got all the attention. Her sports had come first; she got the front seat of the car, and she had her own bedroom. He couldn't stand his sister. He lashed out at her at every opportunity and didn't care that she had a disability. I couldn't understand how I raised a son with zero compassion.

One summer, while he was visiting his father in Oregon, he sent me a text message to tell me he was going to stay in Oregon with his dad. Just like that. "You can just ship me my belongings," he said. OMG…did this just happen? I couldn't believe he said this to me in a text message. Not a phone call, not in person…I was livid. He didn't stay there. He ended up coming home when he realized he wouldn't have his own things.

In the midst of all this, my boss offered me a position in the company that required me to relocate from California to Florida. Big move. After discussing it with my husband, I accepted the position. Allysa did not want to come with us. Well, she did, but she didn't. Her life was already transitioning, and she was fitting into her new life. So, there I was *again*…saying goodbye to my baby girl. Oh, the tears.

We cried so much.

When we got to Florida, Christopher had one more year of high school. He didn't make life easy for me. First, he wanted to graduate early and go back to California. I nipped that in the bud. I told him that he owed me the satisfaction of watching him march and get his diploma. I didn't ask for a lot, but that was the least he could do for me since he had caused so much heartache over the past three years.

I thought I would be able to convince him to stay in Florida and go to college here, but that wasn't the case. He was dying to graduate and go back home, so the time in Florida with my boy was short-lived. As soon as he graduated, he left and went to California. I hugged him hard and cried a lot.

We are true empty nesters. Though my hubby, Lawrence, came into the picture late in the game, he loves my kids as his own, so this affected him as well. Our home was so quiet and empty. Just him, myself, and our dog, Jax. Every day, I went to work, came home, and went to bed, and repeated the process all over again. It was very monotonous and damn near depressing. I had such a hard time "finding myself." Living in a new state didn't help. I had no friends and zero social life here. I hated everything. How was I supposed to live again?

I engrossed myself in work. Not only working my Monday through Friday job, but two side businesses as well. After two years living on the East Coast, my hubby and I finally started to venture out and see a little bit of it. Traveling helped us cope with not having the children around. But what happened when we get home? Back to the empty nest.

Three years later, still missing the kids, I started to venture out on my own—without my husband. He loves his sports and TV, and I just can't be sucked into that lifestyle. I joined an empty nesters' group on Facebook. I made a couple of friends, went to the movies and the gym more often, and most importantly, found my faith in God again. I still get lonely, but now I'm coping with emptiness a lot better. The worst times, however, are still holidays and birthdays. I don't think that will ever go away. My hubby and I talk about moving back to California. I think that will help tremendously so that we are not so lonely. We have another three to four years to finish out our commitments on the East Coast. We will still travel, but we look forward to our move back to California.

Oh! Did I mention that our son asked if he could move back in with us to finish his schooling in Florida? Here we go again! We are very excited, but we also know that we'll have to go through the process of him leaving all over again, so this story is to be continued...

The Coaches' Insight: *Michelle found that her life could be full and enriching. She took giant steps toward getting involved with her community and nurturing friendships through making an action plan and holding herself accountable in achieving it. Michelle is flourishing now by enlisting one small step at a time to fill her life with activities that have brought her joy and happiness.*

Carol's Empty Nest
Traversing the Road to the Empty Nest
Carol (age 56), one child (age 23)

My empty nest began in late August 2012 on the west side of Philadelphia. My 18-year-old daughter, Maggie, started college at Drexel University. I remember the two-and-a-half-hour drive north on I-95 from suburban Washington, DC. She insisted on driving, which was a metaphor in and of itself. I kept looking at her from the passenger seat, awe-struck by her innocent beauty, wondering how we got here. The road we traveled to get her to this point was far longer and more challenging than the trip up I-95.

The trip really began about 14 years earlier. I can remember the exact moment, actually. It was when this beautiful, smart four-year-old stood between her father and me, arms extended fully, to keep the two of us apart. The argument wasn't physical, but it was painful and ugly. It had become an almost daily occurrence, and I couldn't see how it could possibly end. This innocent child, so precious to me, didn't deserve to grow up thinking that this was what a family should be, or what love looks like. She deserved the chance to grow up as I did, in a loving, functional nuclear family. I wanted to be able to model a loving relationship or marriage for her sake, so she would live in an environment of peace and security.

A bitter divorce ensued, but I had a successful career and was able to support her financially and retain our lovely suburban home independently. We were also extremely fortunate that my parents were just a few miles away, and they were there every day after school to welcome her home and prepare dinner until I got home from work. Maggie wanted for nothing, save a traditional nuclear family.

She spent every other weekend and at least one evening a week with her father, but I was still wracked with guilt. I think I tried to make up for it with trips to Florida and DisneyWorld, new clothes and toys, and every activity, including dance and piano lessons, summer day camp, gymnastics, ice skating, and so on. Every evening and the weekends we had together were devoted to her. We read books every night, snuggled together on the sofa watching Disney videos, and danced to music on the stereo. There were trips to the science museum, the pool in the summer, and birthday parties to top any child's dreams.

Still, my angst haunted me. I didn't really have time to pursue relationships of my own, but I still tried, hoping that I'd fall in love with a man and be able to form a stable family for her sake while she was still young enough to accept it. It pains me to this day that I was never able to achieve that, but I'm not sure whether the pain is for me or for her. Probably both.

I was in near constant therapy dealing with anxiety and depression. From the outside, I don't think anyone would have known it. I had a great career with a high-profile position and was well-known in my community as a result. I was financially secure, in good health, and had a supportive family. Yet the constant tension and continued struggles with my ex-husband combined with anxieties over my demanding career and the lack of a significant other, not to mention the stress of single parenthood took a toll on my psyche. Then finally, in 2004, when my daughter was 10, it all came crashing down.

I was fired after filing a lawsuit against my employer for discrimination. I knew that filing such a lawsuit could bring about the end of my career in my field of work, but I felt too strongly not to do so.

I had sworn witnesses and attorneys who believed in my case, and I felt compelled to fight—if not for myself—for women who would follow me. I didn't want other women to suffer the injustice that I had suffered, following years of hard work and struggle to succeed. But I also had an ulterior motive: if the company fired me, I would be unable to find another job in the same city due to a non-compete clause in my contract. This was the only way I could get a family court judge to allow me to relocate—to get away from the toxic environment between my ex and me—something my therapist advised. I know it sounds like a risky, cockamamie way to get out of town, but it was an unusual set of circumstances where the sun, the moon, and the stars had aligned, and I had to take the chance—for my own well-being and that of my daughter.

Sadly, the court sided with the giant corporation and refused to even hear my case. Of course, that added to my angst, feeling that I never got my day in court. But it did free me to move on, and for the next 21 months, I wore out my shoes walking the corridors of Congress, looking for a job. Twice a month, I flew myself down to Washington, DC, trying to change careers (since my previous one was now destroyed).

The stress was suffocating. I had no income, was running out of savings, single-handedly trying to pay the mortgage and raise a child, and find a new career in a new city. Oh, and launch another court case to gain permission to relocate with my daughter. Of course, her father fought tooth and nail to keep us from leaving, even though at this point we were both unemployed and at least one of us needed to land a job! To this day, I thank God that my parents helped as much as they could. I broke down and applied for food stamps and assistance for my daughter's school lunches. It wasn't until years later that she told me how ashamed that made her feel. The memory of those hard times and the effect on her still breaks my heart.

Finally, in the fall of 2005, I got a job offer in DC. The court granted permission for me to take Maggie with me, but said she should be allowed to finish out the school year by living with her father. It killed me to leave her behind. I will never forget leaving her with her father on a miserable day in January, 2006. There we stood in a hard, pouring cold rain on the courthouse steps as daylight faded. She cried, I cried. I could see her eyes saying "Mommy, don't leave me," but I know she didn't want to say that in front of her father. I tried to be strong, but I never felt such wrenching emotional pain before or after. I cried the entire drive that night to Washington.

For the next eight or so months, we talked on the phone every day. I mailed her cheerful letters with dollar bills or other treats inside. I flew back home every other weekend, where we lived in our old house (now on the market) for 48 hours of utter emotional utopia. I rented a lovely apartment in suburban DC and decorated it for the emerging teenager she would soon be. She was elated and couldn't wait to move in.

One day, on one of the weekends she stayed with her father, I was out shopping when my cellphone rang. It was Maggie, and her voice was shaky. That once-in-a-lifetime moment that every girl her age experiences and that every mother wants to share with her daughter had arrived. And I wasn't there. She didn't know what to do, and for whatever reason, it had never occurred to me to provide her with the proper supplies at her father's house. She was not comfortable asking him for help. What was she to do? What was I to do? I so wanted to be with her at this point and felt helpless. How could this happen when I wasn't with her? To her credit, this smart, creative young lady got the idea to call a nearby cousin, who rode her bicycle over to provide the needed supplies. I guess this was the first time I saw my daughter display her ability to solve a problem independently. And that was indeed gratifying, the first proof that I had raised her with the strength to be self-reliant.

Over the next several years, Maggie developed into a teenager with all the concomitant dramas and challenges. She got into trouble at school, started hanging out with kids I didn't like, and frankly, turned into the same strong-headed kid I was at the same age. Her grades dropped. I put her into therapy, which she attended kicking and screaming all the way. I worried what she was doing while I was at work, but she was too old for a babysitter and too young for a job.

Finally, there was a wake-up call. She had gotten into trouble that required a "come to Jesus" moment. I told Maggie to look around at the life she enjoyed with me. We lived in a somewhat upper middle class environment despite the fact that I was a single mother. I explained that while we didn't drive a Mercedes or own private jets (as some of her classmates did!), she was extremely fortunate to have everything she needed—living more comfortably than most Americans in a good neighborhood with great schools. This was a revelation to Maggie. She came to understand that she was surrounded by relatively well-to-do families and as a result, her view of life was skewed. The vast majority of the world did not live the way we did.

"Look around our house, Maggie," I told her. "Everything you see here, every advantage we have, is the result of what I earned. I did not inherit wealth. My parents gave me a loving, secure home and an education. But everything else, I earned through my own hard work. You will not be inheriting anything either. So the choice is yours. You can either follow the path that you're on now and end up in the gutter, or you can clean up your act and live the way to which you've grown accustomed. It's up to you."

Apparently, it had an effect. Maggie dropped some friends, focused on her school work, raised her grades, and (yes, there is a God!) got a full academic scholarship to her first school of choice, Drexel.

And so there we were, on the way to Philadelphia. We unloaded the car, explored the campus, had lunch, and I returned her to the dorm room she was sharing with three other girls. So that was it. The moment we'd been dreaming about, Maggie's freedom from direct parental oversight, had finally arrived. It hit us both. I started walking toward the elevator, and she followed me, bursting into tears. "I love you, Mom." Her face was red and tear-stained. "I love you, too, Maggie, and I'm so proud of you," I told her while we hugged tightly. "I'm only a couple hours away if you need me. Call me as often as you can. Work hard, make me proud, be safe, and have fun. These will be the best years of your life," I told her.

I pushed the button for the elevator, and as the doors closed, I knew our lives were changing forever. This little girl, who held my hand, rode with me on the merry-go-round, and splashed in the pool with me, was on her way. For all those years, it was just her and me against the world. And now, it is—just me.

Can I tell you a secret though? As I walked back to my car with a huge lump in my throat, there was a part of me that was dancing inside. After all the struggles and joys of raising this beautiful daughter, I could finally focus on me. Just me. I could work on losing the weight I'd gained. I could build a social life. Maybe even meet a man. Participate in pastimes I put aside for so many years so I could focus on raising a child. For God's sake, I could even repaint the house without fear of dirty handprints and scuff marks wrought from years of crazy teen parties we hosted.

For four years, I enjoyed the solitude and freedom of being an empty nester. It was made easier by the knowledge that she'd be back frequently for visits. When graduation came in 2016, I felt deeply gratified. This was not just her achievement. It was ours. She asked to move back home for a while to save some money. Of course, I said yes with the condition that there would be an end date. This was for the sake of both of us. Inevitably, there were the occasional squabbles, particularly when she decided to "clean out" my house when I left for a trip. I tried, to no apparent avail, to explain that this was now my house, and she did not have the right to get rid of my stuff, regardless of how useless it appeared to her. This is an ongoing battle.

A couple of months ago, Maggie moved to California to pursue her professional aspirations. It's her first time really living independently, and I'm proud of her for the courage she's displayed, especially since she is self-employed and has to cultivate her own clientele. That means her income is sporadic, and I'm helping financially on a limited basis. So even though she has left the nest, apparently for good this time, she still needs help flying on her own. We talk by phone almost every day, but California is far away and she knows I can't just fly in on a moment's notice. I still help her navigate life from afar, and I know that she still needs me. Frankly, this is largely what keeps me going.

The truth is that I have reached a point where the initial giddiness of the freedom that comes with being an empty nester has worn off. She can't come home often as she did during college, and that year we had living together after her graduation really strengthened our bond as adults. She was and is my best friend. Is that proper? Is it good for us? I have doubts about that.

So right now, I'm struggling to answer some basic life questions. Why am I here? What is my purpose? What is my future? At the moment, I have no job, no life partner, and a dear friend moved away, as did my daughter. I'm floating around with no anchor. I know that sounds really depressing, but I'm trying to look at it as an opportunity to reinvent myself—to figure out what I really want and need at this stage of my life. I fill my days with professional networking and self-care: I work out, practice yoga, try new beauty routines. I see a therapist every week to help me figure out my next step. I talk to my daughter almost daily to provide her with advice and support. This is what provides the most fulfillment.

I lost both of my parents within the last four years, and I think of them every day. I realize I still need them and wonder if that will ever stop. Knowing that reminds me that my daughter will never stop needing me. I'm so proud that she is independently cutting out her own place in life. I vow to myself I will always be there for her, and hopefully someday, for her children. But I also vow to myself that I will find my own purpose, my own joy, now that my primary role as a parent has entered a new phase.

The Coaches' Insight: Carol is taking steps to move forward in her new normal. By working out, networking with professional colleagues, and practicing self-care, she is taking active steps to lean into her new lifestyle. Taking the time to work on ourselves and our needs is the best gift we can give to our children and our continued expanding relationship with them.

Coach Susan's Empty Nest
Still Transitioning into this New Reality...
Coach Susan (age 56), two children (ages 23, 25)

My empty nest journey started the day I dropped my older son Jake off at college in 2011. Let's put this into context though...he was attending the University of Maryland which was literally a 30-minute ride from our home. But there I was, crying like a babbling baby on my drive back home after the big college move-in day. It hit me hard. Life was about to get different, and I wasn't prepared for this on any emotional level. We had been so busy over the years leading up to this event: days and nights filled with homework, activities, college applications, preparing for SAT/ACT tests, going to college counselors, shopping for college stuff—you name it, we did it. Not once along this "preparation for college" journey did I ever think what life would be like once my son left for college; I was just too wrapped up in the preparation. All I kept thinking on that ride home was that this was indeed the beginning of the end; the end of a life I adored, of the life routine to which I became so accustomed. No more seeing him off to school in the morning, sitting around the dinner table talking about our day, saying goodnight to each other as we all turned in for the evening. Life was changing, and I wasn't emotionally prepared.

Fast forward to 2013, and there I was facing the empty nest again. Just as I finally got used to my older son leaving the nest, I was now faced with my younger son Zach leaving for Penn State. Another bittersweet moment. Yet this one hit me harder, right smack between the eyes, as now both my boys were out of the house. The home life that I cherished—that was filled with so many wonderful, crazy, busy moments spent with my two sons—was no more. Done, over, complete. This new normal was so hard for me that when I walked past their empty rooms, it became so difficult that I had to keep their bedroom doors closed; it was too painful. It was a constant reminder that the wonderful phase of our home life together was over. They became visitors in our home, only staying briefly in between college semesters or for holiday breaks.

Jake graduated college in 2015 with his Bachelor of Science in Aerospace Engineering, and I couldn't be prouder. All of his hopes and dreams became a wonderful reality for him as he also had an awesome job to start upon graduating. But this new beginning came with him moving closer to his new job, which was 60 miles away from our home. I was indeed excited for him, and ended up going into super-mom mode—shopping for his work wardrobe, spending endless weekends hunting for an apartment with him, and then shopping like mad for all the stuff he needed to make his apartment a "home." Then came move-in day and once again I was in super-mom mode. I helped him move in furniture and his belongings, set up the apartment, and got him settled, all to make it feel like home for him. I was on auto-mom pilot, constantly going and doing in order to get him settled. But then the fateful moment arrived. It was time for me to leave him; he was finally moved in, all unpacked with furniture set up, with the kitchen adorned and stocked with every item imaginable. As we hugged and said our good-byes, I froze. When I looked at my son, all I could see was a five-year-old boy gazing back at me. How could I possibly leave him alone, I asked myself; he's just a little boy! I remember thinking that I must be a terrible mother for leaving him so far away by himself. He's so young and vulnerable; but no, he's not little— he's a young man, I kept trying to remind myself. Get a grip, Susan! Then my tears welled up, and I kept them at bay as best I could. So there I was once again, not prepared for yet another empty nest moment. Yes, I drove home in tears, as this time I truly realized that he would forever have his own place, and our home would just be a place to visit. The reality of this moment was harsh.

Don't get me wrong, seeing both my boys off to college, and then my oldest son starting his young adult life after graduating were truly proud moments for me; and the proud moments continue as now my youngest son has started his career journey and independent life after graduating college in 2017 with his Bachelor of Science in Energy Business Finance. All of these milestones are the wonderful accumulation of their hard work, and I am so incredibly proud of the amazing young men that they are. I keep telling myself that this is the normal course of life as parents; our "job" is to raise our children to become independent with the ultimate goal that they will have happy, successful, productive lives. It's all bittersweet, as every step they take forward, I feel like I take one step further away from them. The endless days of raising two boys and all the juggling that went with it is over. The reality of not seeing or talking to them on a daily basis is beyond difficult. I know I have to let them have their space on their journeys to adulthood, which means that I now take a backseat in their lives. Yes, I am always there for them with unconditional love, support, and guidance, but I promised myself that I would not be a needy helicopter parent. This is their time to truly test and spread their wings; I have to let them fly.

Some brief background on my journey: When the boys were young, around three and five years old, I left a fulfilling career as a TV/radio producer since my then husband and I decided we could manage financially without my income, and we felt that it was best for the boys to have me stay at home with them. The year that followed this decision was emotionally difficult for me as I always "defined" myself via my career. It took some time for me to be comfortable with my new status—a stay-at-home mom. But in time, I embraced it, and just as I did in my career, I gave it my all, and ended up loving every second of it, even the crazy moments. I became involved in their school, volunteered on committees and in the classroom, was the constant "field trip mom," and was there for all their extra-curricular activities, sporting events, endless nights assisting with homework and school projects. You name it, I was there along-side them...assisting, listening, supporting, guiding, and cheering them on.

But then in 2005 our lives changed due to my divorce from their dad; it was difficult to say the least. But we navigated it, and some days were indeed harder than others. For me, it was a never-ending roller coaster of emo-tions, some of which I wish I kept to my-self. In 2006, I reentered the workforce as a recruiter, which was then followed by going back to college to earn my Master's in Human Resource Management, followed by my Mas-ter's in Business Administration, and then my

Life/Career Coach certification. It was several years of growing my new career as an HR Professional (my mid-life reinvention), juggling college studies, maintaining a home, and raising two teenage boys. I will not lie; some days were indeed a "crash and burn" day—total exhaustion from it all. There were days when I wish didn't feel so rushed and others that sucked the life out of me, but as exhausting as those days were, I now long for them. I miss the boys' energy that filled my home as well as the chaos that came with it; I just miss seeing my boys every day.

In 2013, I lost my dad due to a horrific stroke. Words can't even begin to describe my emotions on his passing. What stung the most is that we finally achieved an amazing father-daughter relationship after having a turbulent relationship during my adolescent years, which were filled with numerous arguments—mostly due to his ill health and subsequent short temper, but peppered by me being a bitchy teenager fighting for independence. When I reentered the workforce in 2006, my father became a true source of support and care for my boys. He or my mom would be at my home after school to greet the boys or pick them up from the school bus if needed while I was at work. The bond that grew between my dad and my boys was simply immeasurable; they adored him, and he adored them. So yes, his death rattled any sense of stability I finally felt in my life, as both my boys were away at college, and I finally started to come to terms with my empty nest. All of this became a double dose of grief for me—missing my boys and the life we had, and then missing my dad. I was unable to cope with it all, especially my dad's death, and ended up going to counseling because I couldn't navigate through the horrible raw world of grief. It helped, but not as much as I had hoped, as grief is a process that takes time. During this period, I remembered that my dad had written heaps of notes about his life, specifically how he fled the Nazis and immigrated to America during the Holocaust as a young Hasidic boy. I decided to dive into his notes to learn more about my dad, put it all together as a story, and edit it so that it could become a book for the family, especially for my boys. I spent a year on this project, and it not only brought me peace, but I found that through writing/editing my dad's story, it was truly a healing process for me. In 2015, I ended up self-publishing my dad's story. So you see, writing is a bit of therapy for me, which is why writing about my empty nest experience is a form of healing now. I know this, too, is a process of navigating my emotions in order to find a way to optimistically move forward with my "new normal."

During the unraveling of my little nest, my loneliness was amplified because my life partner, Bill, lived over 1,000 miles away from me in Florida. We kept a long distance relationship as I vowed to stay in Maryland until my boys were done with college. This long-distance relationship lasted for over a decade, but we managed. In December 2016, I sold my beloved Maryland home in which I raised two amazing young men, the home that Bill spent months renovating for us that was then filled with too many memories to count. But it was time. My alimony was ending, and I could no longer afford my home, which was purchased knowing that it would be for a defined timeframe. The home was close to my parents, in the boy's school district, close to their friends, and in a neighborhood that I knew would provide them with a great life after the divorce. But the time had come to move; and yes, I was moving to Florida to be with Bill. During the six months leading up to selling the house and the subsequent move, I went into hyper downsizing mode. I was too busy to think of, or even know, what emotions might be brewing deep down inside of me regarding this life-altering decision of mine—emotions that didn't surface until months after I moved to Florida. I worked tirelessly to pack, declutter, toss, and donate all things throughout the house. I prepared the house for sale; I had my boys pack and clean out their rooms. It was a non-stop packing and downsizing production—full steam ahead, giving little thought to the emotions attached to the process. But the emotions did sneak in. The first wave started when the boys' rooms became totally void of any memory of them, as all their possessions were gone. The second wave of emotions came when I sold their bedroom furniture, which they had since they were each two years old. I remember sitting between both of their rooms, staring at total emptiness and crying relentlessly; it felt as though there was no memory of "us" anymore. The memories of their childhood and all of our times together flooded through me like wildfire, all but consuming me. My heart tore into a million pieces; I wanted it all to stop. I wanted our nest put back together! I kept telling myself, "Just breathe; you've got this." This is part of the empty nest, or should I say, the emptying of the nest process. Whatever it was, I didn't want it.

It is now almost one year after my move to Florida to be with Bill and start our life together. I have good days and bad days; the empty nest is still a work in progress for me. I still grieve for the life I had when it was my boys and me together under the same roof. Don't get me wrong; I'm happy to finally be living with Bill, and I know that even if I had stayed in Maryland, neither boy would be living with me. So either way, whether it was Florida or Maryland, life would be different. I still struggle with the fact that it was I who moved away from our home state as it's more often the child who moves and not the parent. I find comfort in my decision when I see my friends who have also moved away from their children to start their new empty nest phase in life, and see that they still have wonderful, close relationships with their children despite the distance. All I can say is thank goodness for modern technology, as texting has become one of my lifelines with my boys.

So yes, the emptying of the nest is a process that I wasn't emotionally prepared for. It's been a journey since the day that my oldest son left for college in 2011. I truly wish someone had prepared me for the emotions attached to this journey, which is probably why I have chosen to write about it, both as a mom and as a life coach. Life is a series of transitions—some good, some bad, some just plain difficult. Life is about moving forward, and to do so, you have to be nimble and learn how to navigate the changes; it's a matter of choice on how we deal with the emotions we face during any life-changing process. I'm learning to navigate and accept my new normal, which now consists of the occasional phone calls, emails, and text messages, as well as visits with my boys. No, it is not the same as living under one roof together. I embrace all the wonderful past childhood memories of raising my boys with deep gratitude and love, and try to remain optimistic for what the future holds. I am a person of "reinvention" based on how I created and pursued a successful and fulfilling midlife career change, and I know that I have the ability to do the same with redefining my new normal as an empty nester.

The Coaches' Insight: Susan came to embrace her current situation by allowing herself to go through all of the five phases of grief. She was present to the feelings that came up for her. As a result of all of these struggles, Susan came out even stronger than before. She became a person of reinvention. She embraced her new normal and knew that her life as she once knew it had forever changed, but she also recognized that she had changed beautifully alongside it.

Coach Briget's Empty Nest
The Biggest Transition of Your Life, Hold On...
Coach Briget (age 60), two children (ages 29, 30)

I knew this day would someday come. When it finally arrived, my daughters were ready, but I was absolutely not prepared and not there yet. So this is my story.

An empty nest. What a picture. A round circular bed of plain sticks with a few leaves thrown in for good measure. No one in the nest to keep you warm. That is where I found myself after my daughters left for college, and my husband asked me for a divorce after 22 years of marriage. I have to say, that was a tall order for which I was honestly unprepared. Who knew? Completely alone in the nest. No one to snuggle with, share my day with or share a meal. Nada, zero, zippy. Wow, 50 years old and alone. Instead of asking, "Why me, Lord?" I asked, "What now, Lord?" Now what do I do with my time, my feelings, my work, and my new life? My life was totally dedicated to my family and my marriage. Now my daughters were going off to find their own path in this world, and at the same time, I had to find a new path to journey—only this time, on my own.

So what did I do? It always comes down to a fundamental choice. You either sit there and feel sorry for yourself and become incredibly bitter, or you choose a different path. Not the one you planned, but the one you were dealt. I honestly do not know which was harder, my children leaving or my husband. Either way, my family as I had come to know it changed on a dime. I needed to change with it or become miserable, lonely, and of no use to anyone. So this is what I did. I decided I needed to start fresh, so I left my home behind and looked for a new home in a different neighborhood.

My firstborn daughter, Maureen, left the nest at the age of 18, traveling six hours away to go to college. I drove her there with a car chock full of dorm room supplies, bedding, towels, and personal items. My daughter could not wait and was incredibly excited, anticipating this newfound freedom.

Actually dropping Maureen off at school for the first time was very similar to when I dropped her off at kindergarten on the first day. It was a feeling of believing that no one could possibly know your child the way that you do. A feeling that only you know what her wants and needs are. Only you know what is best for her. It is quite sobering when you drop them off at college and realize that your child is now an adult. In the back of your mind you remember that she has been raised to act and think for herself—all part of the human condition. Only this time, she is totally on her own. You want her to make the best decisions with what life may throw her way.

We arrived at the University, which was absolutely beautiful—a large campus set in the beautiful mountains. I remember arriving. That day was filled with lots of freshmen who were anxiously awaiting newfound freedom. The school had an incredible system to get them prepared for their first experience away from home. The parents met with the school officials and were led on a tour of the campus, and then it was time for us to get in our cars and drive our kids up to the dorm. At that point, they had several senior students who knew the drill. One helped unload the car. The next helped to bring the students belongings into the room. Another one was there for IT concerns to hook up their computers and WiFi. It all happened so fast. I had 18 years with my daughter, and this transition to her new home in the college dorm took 7.5 minutes. Wow… At that point, we went to a final meeting in the school auditorium, where the president of the university welcomed the parents. He gave us a brief history of the university, letting us know that our children were in excellent hands and that they would receive an outstanding education. I remember his last words before I drove back to Virginia. "We will take it from here."

When I drove back home, it was eerily quiet. My child had entered adulthood and was receiving an incredible education. "She will take it from here," I kept telling myself.

Maureen went off to college in 2005, and I knew my daughter Tori was soon to follow. At that time, I had a wonderful work support group that consisted of two moms who were experiencing the very same thing. The three of us scheduled empty nest lunches outside the office to discuss our incredible sadness as well as coping strategies that we could try. We realized that this was new to all of us, and it was not going to be an easy road to travel.

The most difficult emotions that I did not anticipate were the loneliness and sadness that came with the realization that my daughter was on her own and would not return home, with the exception of holidays and summer vacations, for the next four years. But my youngest daughter was in her senior year of high school. That left us crazy busy, but the void of not having my oldest at home changed the dynamics, and new adjustments had to be made.

During this time, my sisters and brothers were experiencing their children going off to college. There was comfort in knowing that I was not alone. I come from a large Irish Catholic family, so being able to talk to my two brothers and three sisters about this was very comforting. Still, even having close siblings going through this at the same time, I soon realized that this was an individual journey. It is similar to grieving, which is not a family activity; grieving is a solo activity. No one can possibly know what is racing through your heart and mind at any given point in time.

So how does a mom cope when her child goes off to college? I was very active in my church, in my neighborhood, and at work. I went out with fellow moms who were experiencing the same thing. On the one hand, it was so difficult for our children to go off and be on their own. On the other hand, when they came home for a break, familiar scenes played out: wet towels left at the end of the bed; bedrooms became very messy; their long beautiful hair was left behind in the bathroom sink and shower; they came home late at night. It's funny—when they return to college, the house seems a lot quieter and better organized.

Now that I have been through the empty nest, I would tell my younger self to relax and laugh more, stress less, and enjoy the little things in life. After all, it is the little things that actually have the biggest impact on our lives.

I had often thought that God made our children leaving the nest a little easier by creating teenagers! This rite of passage of being a teenager lends itself to stretching the limits of parenthood. The daily dance of going from an adolescent to an adult stretches the once very closely adhered to boundaries.

After my daughters had been out of the nest for a while, I vividly remembered how important it was to share my feelings with close friends. I had two great friends whom I walked with early on Saturday mornings. We walked and prayed on a two-mile country road that we lovingly called "The Healing Road." We talked about our sadness and our difficult journey for the first two miles, then we turned around and took turns praying for one another during the second two miles. I honestly do not know what I would have done during this phase of my life had it not been for my friends. We were all going through a difficult time, each with its own set of hardships and fears, and we allowed ourselves to be downright vulnerable and scared together in the paths of our lives that were ahead. Those walks were such a significant time in my journey. They helped me to sort things out. They helped me to see things more clearly. They helped me to know that I was absolutely not alone. Each and every one of us goes through trials in this life. Each and every one of us goes through times where we see no way out—where we long for "the way things used to be." We then romanticize those times and make them much larger than they actually ever were. By walking, talking, sharing, and most importantly praying, I was able to come through to the other side of sadness that my daughters and my husband were gone. Instead of seeing myself as a woman who was lost, scared, and intimidated by what was to come in my future, I saw things for what they really were. I was able to see things in a brand new light and wake myself up to the "possibility" that it was going to work out, and the "possibility" that I would come out stronger, more confident, more determined, and more loving than I could have ever imagined.

So how did I get there? I started out from a focal point of forgiveness once all the dust settled. By forgiving, I was able to set my heart free. Did that mean that all was roses from that point on? Absolutely not. What it did was free my heart to find love where I used to see only hurt and loss. It opened my heart to other people and opportunities that otherwise would have never been there. I know that going through the process and looking for God's hand in all of it was my saving grace. Taking someone who felt broken, totally alone, and scared, and then opening that person up to a new way of life and of living, was all from God. I know I could not have done this on my own. It was too personal, too real, too painful.

As in photography, it is all about the angles from which you view things. It is about knowing where the focal point lies. It is about the rule of thirds. New patterns and new traditions are now a daily part of my life. I embrace change where before I would run from it. I am trying new things that I would have never done before. I even went parasailing in Jamaica with my daughter Tori, and believe me, I would have never attempted that before. Being single gave me the courage to step out and step up. The empty nest gave me a totally new perspective. We raised our daughters not only to fly, but to soar. They could not do that unless we let them go and try their wings alone. They stumbled and fell many times, but they got back up even stronger.

My ex-husband is now remarried to a beautiful woman who loves my children and my two grandchildren dearly. I realized that by truly loving someone, you actually want that person to be happy. My ex-husband is very happy in his marriage and in his life. That brings me comfort.

With my daughters, having the empty nest made me realize that they are amazingly strong, independent women. They have love in their lives and they challenge themselves in their work and in their personal lives. That is what we raised them to do. I recognize that I cannot stop that train. I can't hold on to the high school years where we ran from one activity to another. I came to the realization that I am no longer actively parenting. That does not mean that my role of being a parent is diminished in any way. It just means that I am not involved in their day-to-day decisions. What helped me was time and space. Giving my daughters room to grow and to make their own mistakes—no matter how painful—and to fall, has been the hardest and most rewarding thing I have ever done. When I think back to leaving my parents' house at age 18, my mother did the same thing. She trusted me to fly and soar on my own. I made my own decisions and my own choices in college. Since my parents had prepared me along the way, I was comfortable and confident when I went away to school. I wanted to give that same gift to my daughters.

So what to do from here? How do you persuade yourself to move forward and find something positive about the situation? Well, for me, I needed to do it one hour at a time and then progress to one day at a time. It was similar to what my daughters were doing, just navigating through unchartered territory. The difference was they were extremely excited about it and I was scared to death...

But a funny thing happened to me during this time. I learned several things about myself. I learned that keeping in touch with my daughters while they were at school was important. It was, however, very different. I no longer knew their day-to-day plans as well as I once did. I learned that I was not a fragile flower that would just wither and die on the vine. I learned that I have true grit; I am resourceful, strong, and resilient. This had never happened to me before. It was all new, but I started to come out on the other side. My daughters were also in a situation that was new to them. All of us had to learn to navigate the world in a different way. That is the key. It was not impossible, nor unbearable. It was just…different.

For so many years, I had given all of my time and devotion to my beautiful family. Then it was my turn to spread my wings to fly. We all have a choice at this juncture: do we want to fly, or do we want to soar? I emphatically have chosen to soar. I wanted to take all that life had to offer and create a new sacred space for myself in order to grow as a mother, a woman, a manager at work, a friend, and a Christian woman in this world that desperately needs to see the love of Jesus all around us. So this is a new chapter in my life. I am eager to turn the page and read what lies ahead.

The Coaches' Insight: *Briget's journey is one of realizing the need to find and create a new direction, which was fueled with hope and forgiveness. Through self-reflection and refocusing, she gained motivation to create a new and wonderful enriching life for herself.*

Insights from Discussions with Story Contributors and Other Empty Nesters

In reading through our story contributors' essays and speaking to other Empty Nesters, we identified a few key topics, as well as common threads within each topic. We are delighted to share them, as well as our coaching insights, which are based on our perspective of the responses.

Does being a hyper-involved parent make the Empty Nest a harder transition? In speaking to several moms, we noticed that this might be the case, as an overwhelming number of them responded with "Yes, it does make this a harder transition." This doesn't mean it was wrong to be super involved in your child's life, but it may help to understand the emotions of emptiness, as there is now a huge void in how you once spent your time.

Empty Nester Response: I dedicated my

entire life to my children and am now at a loss on how to remain involved with them (as well as move forward) now that they are out of the house and on their own.

Coaching Insight: This is a great time to find new ways to remain involved with your child while respecting his or her need for independence. Depending on your child, your new level of involvement will need to be determined, and it's absolutely okay to ask them what feels right! Find the balance of what fits your circumstances with your child; this might include some trial and error, but you will find the balance that works for both of you. Unfortunately, there isn't a "one size fits all" here, and sometimes what works with one child doesn't necessarily work well with another. Each child is unique in his or her desire for independence, and we suggest using that to navigate the comfort level of your involvement in their lives; let their social cues guide you. Remember to be patient with the process and your emotions; sometimes a bit more space is required for the natural progression of this new relationship to occur.

We've found in our own experiences that sometimes taking a step back is needed so that we don't appear to smother our children because of our own need to remain involved. It's difficult, but remember when you were young and setting out on your own—and didn't want your parents hovering? Well, it's the same thing for many of us during this time now—so just remember your younger self at this time.

Does being a stay-at-home mom (SAHM) increase the emotions of the Empty Nest? We did find that some women who were SAHMs had an increased sense of emptiness, as well as questioned "who they were" after their child/children left the nest. The emptiness that they felt from the void was not much different than non-SAHMs, but there was a great sense of "who am I" voiced by the SAHMs. This helps to provide some insight regarding the emotional struggle we face with the Empty Nest.

> **Empty Nester Response**: I created my entire life around being a SAHM and am now struggling with how to create a new life for myself.

Coaching Insight: Many women said that despite the emptiness they feel now, as well as their loss of personal identity (as many stopped or didn't have a career outside the home), that they would not have changed a thing since being a SAHM was their choice. This was wonderful insight; despite the "who am I" emotions from some of the SAHMs, most were happy with their choice. They just realized that they might have a bit more of a challenge now, regarding both reinventing themselves as well as simultaneously dealing with the Empty Nest. We all have choices; some choose to juggle a career and motherhood, and some choose full-time motherhood as their career. Rather than ponder what was given up in terms of a career in order to be a SAHM, think instead about the possibilities of the future since we can't go back in time to change the present circumstances. This is your time to explore opportunities (paid/unpaid/volunteer) that interest you. Consider this a great chance to explore who you are, as well as a chance to possibly start a new career.

What would you tell your younger self in preparing for the Empty Nest? And is there any way to truly prepare? This question provided the greatest amount of responses, which we believe are based on one's ability to transition into the Empty Nest phase, coupled with their unique set of circumstances (i.e., divorced, happy marriage, SAHM, non-SAHM, rewarding career/job, family support, etc.)

> **Empty Nester Response**: I wish I had focused more on my husband/spouse while raising my kids, as in the end, it is now just the two of us, and we are struggling to reconnect.
>
> **Coaching Insight**: It's never too late to reconnect with your spouse/significant other. Take this time to rekindle your relationship, and invest your time like you did when you first met. If needed, reach out to ask for professional help in order to restore your relationship. Try to remember what attracted you to each other when you first met, and use that as a basis to grow and get to know each other again.
>
> **Empty Nester Response**: I wish I hadn't

stopped doing the things that interested me, such as hobbies and interests outside of home life.

Coaching Insight: The good news is that it's not too late, and now you have the gift of time to reconnect with your interests, as well as explore new interests. Try to look at this newfound time as a gift to reconnect with who you are and what interests you. This exploration will help fill any void you are feeling, and might even surprise you with renewed feelings of hope and positivity.

Empty Nester Response: I wish I hadn't stopped my career, as well as I wish I had a career.

Coaching Insight: Understanding that this is not an easy, overnight fix, there are ways you can resume/reinvent your career. If you've been out of the workforce for a while, you may want to work with a career coach or find a mentor to assist in the process. Taking the time to first explore "what makes you tick" is important when seeking out new jobs/opportunities. Fortunately, we can be resourceful women in rebuilding and reinventing ourselves.

Empty Nester Response: Take more time to just enjoy the kids growing up; create more memories, take more pictures—don't sweat the little stuff!

Coaching Insight: Life is filled with incredible opportunities to create powerful memories. This is so important because time marches on. We recommend being mindful of living in the present moment. By learning to appreciate the time we have with our children, whether it's the mundane day-in and day-out stuff, or family-filled vacations, they are all wonderful snippets of treasured memories. Sure, it's easy to say don't sweat the small stuff—we all probably had those moments of the screaming toddler and wished for those crazy years to end. But now looking back, many would give anything for those moments because they miss their kids so much. So the basic, simplistic message is to learn to live, love, and appreciate the present moment—it all goes by in a flash, so don't wish them away. Always be creating memories! That is what helps in looking back with love and gratitude while moving forward to shape your future Empty Nest journey. And don't stop there—there are tons of new memories to create with your independent adult child (and possibly grandchildren).

Empty Nester Response: I wouldn't have changed anything!

Coaching Insight: Wow! This was amazing—and this statement cut across many situations—the working mom as well as the stay-at-home mom. For the working moms, they were happy with the choices they made in balancing kids, family, and work. For the stay-at-home moms, many said they would not change anything, as focusing solely on their children (some homeschooled their children) was their priority and the time spent was priceless. It's all about choices, and it's refreshing to hear that many women are at peace with the choices they made, as it appears to foster a more positive outlook with the Empty Nest phase that follows.

Observations About
the Empty Nest

So what is the Empty Nest all about? Is it a point in time that defines how your home life is now, which is void of having your children live with you? Probably.

But what about the concept of *"emptying the nest?"* As parents, we prepare our children to learn independence in the hope that one day they will be able to navigate the world as thriving independent adults. This starts in the toddler years as children become aware of their own abilities, and continues to expand throughout adolescence as they become more capable. If we think about it, we cheer them on when they learn to walk, talk, feed, and dress themselves. We say goodbye to them with a tear in our eye on that first day of pre-school or kindergarten, or possibly daycare for mothers returning to work. The bird leaving the nest is indeed in stages. This follows additional forms of separation as the child grows, such as attending sleep-away camp, going out with friends without parental supervision, or simply taking that first solo car ride with their new driver's license.

So maybe if we view the Empty Nest as a process rather than a single point in time, we would be better emotionally prepared for the finale? Yes, the nest is empty when the kids have moved out, and for some it becomes an emotionally overwhelming and life-altering situation. There is no singular best way to deal with the emotions of the Empty Nest since we are all individuals with unique circumstances. Perhaps the ability to deal with these emotions, whether they be emptiness, loss, sadness, or fear is based on one's ability to navigate change. The saying goes, "Change is inevitable." With this in mind, we can't stop the inevitable from happening, but we can learn to deal with the emotions that come with it, as well as ways to positively move forward, and even prepare ourselves for it.

We get so caught up in the daily routine of "doing" that we never give proper thought to the end result, which is our kids leaving us to start their own lives. But if someone had prepared us along the way, we would have not been so blind-sided with a barrage of emotions that are difficult to control. We prepare them to leave the nest, so why not prepare ourselves? Hindsight is 20/20, and there are many "would haves and should haves" that come up at this new dawn.

From our observations, some are able to cope better than others with significant life transitions, such as the Empty Nest; yet there is no rhyme or reason as to who is able to cope better. We hear (and know from our coaching and personal experiences) that it is a huge sense of loss—of our identity as a mom. This means that we need to find new and creative ways to redefine motherhood and move forward in this new paradigm.

A Look Through the Coaching Lens

Routines and circumstances change, and all of a sudden, your life has drastically taken on a new trajectory. This can go one of two ways. We can embrace the change as a beautiful part of the various stages and passages of life, or we can feel stuck, lonely, sad, and that there are no more exciting activities to keep us fulfilled. The important thing to remember is… *we* get to choose. *We* get to decide. *We* get to direct our thoughts in any direction *we* want.

So how do we go from here to there when our whole world as we have known it for the past 18 years suddenly comes to a screeching halt? First, we continue to breathe. We continue to take one hour at a time, one day at a time, and gently move forward. Our days are the same; it is only what we decide to fill them with that has changed.

As mothers and coaches, we went through all five stages of grief while experiencing the loss of our children leaving the nest:

1. **Denial**: Can this really be happening? Are our children leaving the nest, or is this just a bad dream?
2. **Anger**: Why did this have to happen? This is incredibly unfair.
3. **Bargaining**: Would give anything to have the family unit whole and complete again.
4. **Depression**: Just need time to figure this all out and come up with a plan to move forward.
5. **Acceptance**: At this point, you realize that this is reality. You cannot turn back the hands of time; you need to accept it for what it is and make the best plans for the future that you can.

These stages of grief come and go at various times and in various scenarios, and sometimes they are not even linear. Our minds need to fully appreciate all that has occurred around us to get grounded, make a plan, and recognize that we will not only survive, we will thrive.

Change the way you look at things, and the things you look at will change.

~ Buddhist Proverb

Where Do We Go From Here?

First things first: recognize where you are. That may not come easy with all of the emotions swirling around inside of you and the fact that you were so accustomed to having every minute of every day consumed with the children's activities. You may find one or more of the following insights work well for you.

1. **Be kind to yourself**. Give yourself the time and space to feel every emotion without judgment. Recognize the wonderful accomplishments you have made as a loving and supportive parent.

2. **Replace negativity with positivity**. When a negative thought tries to overtake you, recognize it and replace it with something positive. Your thoughts have real power.

3. **Don't be afraid to reach out**. While you may feel isolated, you have family and/or friends who will listen to you. You may consider starting a journal, which

often helps people work through their thoughts. If you continue to struggle, seek the advice of a professional.

4. **Set realistic expectations**. Your life situation has changed, and you need to adapt your expectations accordingly. Communicate with your child who has left the nest, but try not to make demands. Put yourself in their shoes and remember how you felt when you left the nest. Listen to each other, and seek common ground that meets everyone's needs.

5. **Be open to change**. The Empty Nest journey is not a "one size fits all" process, and much of it depends on the relationship you had with your child before he/she left the nest. If you accept that something that worked last month needs to work differently now, you'll save yourself frustration and heartache.

6. **Rediscover yourself**. Whether it's your first or last child leaving the nest, recognize the opportunity to use your time to *your* best advantage. Rekindle your relationship with your spouse or

significant other if you have one. Spend time together traveling or pursuing hobbies that have fallen by the wayside. If you're single, reconnect with family members and friends. Explore new activities. Commit yourself to something that interests *you*.

7. **Practice "I AM" statements**. You're a parent, but you're so much more than that. Consider your interests and core values, and shift your self-identification to include things that aren't related to being a parent.

8. **Launch an Empty Nest Companions group**. Identify other empty nesters in your area and launch a group that can provide loving support to its members. There is strength in companionship with people in similar situations.

Just when the caterpillar thought the world was over, it became a butterfly.

~ English Proverb

Closing Thoughts by Coaches Susan and Briget

For us, the Empty Nest visual perfectly depicts the transition phase of when our children left our homes, a home void of our children. We both experienced the Empty Nest at different times, yet we had similar feelings. It left us feeling vulnerable and alone with feelings that were almost indescribable to anyone who had never experienced this transition. It seemed as if everyone else was getting on with their busy lives while ours were running in slow motion. We believed that it was important for us to feel and address our feelings to realize that we had lots of living ahead of us, which not only helped during this phase but was the inspiration of this book. We each navigated our way out of the depths of the Empty Nest via our own processes, and found that when we were stronger, our family was stronger. We hope that this book sheds a little light on the great possibilities that are ahead of you and your family, and wish you all the best on this journey. All wonderful things are indeed possible!

You are still mom. You will *never* stop being mom. The only change is the capacity in which you experience being a mom. You have so many blessings right in front of you. Enjoy them and use them to your advantage every day. Gift your children with the knowledge that you not only survived this journey, but you set sail and became totally alive during it.

You are still you…a little older, a lot wiser, and more engaged than ever in the world around you. Welcome to your promotion to this new chapter of your life!

About the Authors

Susan Gross is a Certified Professional Coach (CPC) and Energy Leadership Index Master Practitioner (ELIMP) from the Institute for Professional Excellence in Coaching (IPEC); as well as a SHRM-CP (Society for Human Resource ManagementCertified Professional) and Professional in Human Resources (PHR) through HRCI. Susan started in the Human Resource/Recruiting field in 2006 upon re-entering the workforce after her divorce and several years as a stay-at-home mom. As an executive search recruiter, she focused in the creative market, a space that was familiar to her based on an extensive 15-year background in marketing/advertising as a TV and radio broadcast producer. Upon obtaining her Master's in Human Resource Management followed by an MBA in 2010, she began working as a Human Resource Professional. Susan is also the co-author of "Tibi's Journey From Nyirbator to America," her father's memoir of surviving the Holocaust. When she is not working, she enjoys spending time with family and friends, going to the beach, practicing yoga, and serving as a volunteer career coach for recent college graduates. Susan has two sons, Jake and Zach, and currently resides in Florida.

Briget Bishop is a Certified Professional Life Coach who throws a life jacket to women who are overwhelmed by one or more of a variety of life circumstances, from dread in their marriages to dissatisfaction in the workplace. She empowers her clients to navigate successfully through these murky waters and life challenges. With more than 33 years of experience in Nursing, Information Technology, Coaching and Mentoring, Briget brings a wealth of practical knowledge to her coaching work. She received an MBA from Averett University, a Bachelor's of Science Degree in Nursing from Western Connecticut State University, and a certification as a Certified Professional Coach and Energy Leadership Index Master Practitioner from the Institute for Professional Excellence in Coaching, which is recognized by the International Coaching Federation. When she isn't working, Briget enjoys volunteering at two local organizations,

The House of Mercy and Commissioned by Christ. A Northern Virginia resident, she enjoys spending time with daughters Maureen and Tori, as well as two grandchildren, Jack and Evelynn.

If you would like to contact Susan and Briget, please email us at: EmptyNestCompanion@gmail.com

About the Editor

Nancy Griffin-Bonnaire, editor, is a promotional copywriter and professional copyeditor who continually seeks to better her own writing and gets great satisfaction helping others improve theirs. She can be reached through her website, www.markmywordsinc.com.

The Empty Nest Companion
Journal Notes

...a little place to write your thoughts...

How are you navigating the transition to your Empty Nest?

_____

_____

_____

_____

_____

_____

_____

_____

_____

_____

_____

How are you navigating the transition to your Empty Nest?

_____

_____

_____

_____

_____

_____

_____

_____

_____

_____

_____

_____

*What ways are you staying connected with
your child/children…do they work?
If not, what can be adjusted and how?*

_____

_____

_____

_____

_____

_____

_____

_____

_____

_____

_____

*What ways are you staying connected with
your child/children...do they work?
If not, what can be adjusted and how?*

What ways are you moving forward in your life to find the real "you"?
This can possibly be a new job, volunteering, forming new friendships, rekindling old friendships, a new hobby, etc.

_____

_____

_____

_____

_____

_____

_____

_____

_____

_____

What ways are you moving forward in your life to find the real "you"?
This can possibly be a new job, volunteering, forming new friendships, rekindling old friendships, a new hobby, etc.

What are some positive aspects of being an Empty Nester for you?

_____

_____

_____

_____

_____

_____

_____

_____

_____

_____

_____

What are some positive aspects of being an Empty Nester for you?

_____

_____

_____

_____

_____

_____

_____

_____

_____

_____

_____

What isn't working for you as an Empty Nester, and how can you change it? List action items to help you focus and move forward with these changes:

_____

_____

_____

_____

_____

_____

_____

_____

_____

_____

What isn't working for you as an Empty Nester, and how can you change it? List action items to help you focus and move forward with these changes:

_____

_____

_____

_____

_____

_____

_____

_____

_____

_____

Made in the USA
Las Vegas, NV
08 September 2022